Mastering Xcode: A Developer's Journey

Kameron Hussain and Frahaan Hussain

Published by Sonar Publishing, 2024.

While every precaution has been taken in the preparation of this book, the publisher assumes no responsibility for errors or omissions, or for damages resulting from the use of the information contained herein.

MASTERING XCODE: A DEVELOPER'S JOURNEY

First edition. January 27, 2024.

ISBN: 979-8224794133

Written by Kameron Hussain and Frahaan Hussain.

Table of Contents

Section 14.1: Performance Optimization Techniques

1. Profiling Your App

2. Memory Management

3. Optimizing User Interface (UI)

4. Background Processing

5. Reducing Network Usage

6. Optimizing Algorithms and Data Structures

7. Code Profiling

8. Efficient Resource Management

9. Testing and Benchmarking

10. App Thinning and Optimization Strategies

Section 14.2: Efficient Memory Usage

1. Automatic Reference Counting (ARC)

2. Use Structs When Appropriate

3. Managing Caches

4. Lazy Loading

5. Deallocating Unused Objects

6. Avoid Strong Reference Cycles

7. Monitoring Memory Usage

Section 14.3: Optimizing CPU and Battery Usage

1. Use Background Tasks Wisely

2. Threading and Concurrency

3. Energy Profiling with Instruments

4. Idle Timers and Background Modes

5. Network Efficiency

6. Core Location and GPS

7. Optimize Animations

8. Background Audio and Media Playback

9. Power Monitoring

10. Regularly Test on Low-End Devices

Section 14.4: Network Performance Tuning

1. Use Efficient Data Formats

2. Pagination and Lazy Loading

3. Caching

4. Background Fetching

5. Optimize Images

6. Reduce Network Requests

7. Monitor and Handle Connectivity Changes

8. Error Handling and Retries

9. Optimize for Cellular Data Usage

2. Define Clear Goals

3. Map Out User Journeys

4. Simplify Navigation

5. Use Visual Cues

6. Consistent Layout and Design

7. Feedback and Confirmation

8. Error Handling

9. User Testing

10. Optimize for Mobile

11. Onboarding

12. Analytics and Monitoring

13. Personalization

Chapter 16: Security and Privacy in Apps

Section 16.1: Implementing Security Best Practices

Section 16.2: Data Encryption and Secure Storage

1. Keychain Services

2. File-Based Encryption

3. Data Transmission

4. Regular Data Purging

5. Secure Data Backup

6. Strong Authentication

Section 16.3: Network Security and API Protection

1. Secure Communication

2. Certificate Pinning

3. OAuth and API Tokens

4. Rate Limiting and Access Control

5. Data Validation

6. API Versioning

7. Security Headers

Section 16.4: Privacy Policies and User Data

1. Privacy Policy

2. Transparency

3. Data Minimization

4. Consent

5. Data Security

6. Data Retention

7. User Rights

8. Third-Party Services

9. Regular Updates

10. Compliance

Chapter 1: Introduction to Xcode

1.1. The Evolution of Xcode: A Brief History

Xcode, Apple's integrated development environment (IDE), has undergone significant evolution since its inception. Understanding its history provides context for the robust development environment it has become today.

Early Beginnings

Xcode originated as Project Builder in the late 1990s when Apple transitioned to Mac OS X. Initially, it was a separate development tool that coexisted with CodeWarrior, a popular Mac development environment at the time. Project Builder laid the foundation for what would later become Xcode.

Xcode's Birth

With the release of Mac OS X 10.0, Project Builder evolved into Xcode. Apple integrated various development tools and technologies into a single cohesive platform, simplifying the development process for macOS and iOS applications. Xcode's debut marked the beginning of a new era for Apple developers.

Interface Builder Integration

Xcode 2.0, introduced in 2005, brought Interface Builder into the Xcode package. This integration allowed developers to design user interfaces seamlessly alongside their code. The combination of Interface Builder and Xcode streamlined app development and significantly improved the user interface design experience.

The App Store Era

Xcode played a pivotal role in the success of the App Store, which launched in 2008. With the advent of iOS, Xcode became the primary IDE for developing applications for iPhone and iPad. Its evolution continued with features tailored for iOS app development.

Swift Language

In 2014, Apple introduced the Swift programming language, and Xcode played a central role in its adoption. The IDE provided powerful tools for Swift development, including code completion, error checking, and debugging support. This marked a major milestone in Xcode's history.

Modern Development

Today, Xcode continues to evolve, offering support for macOS, iOS, watchOS, and tvOS development. It incorporates a wide range of features such as Interface Builder, Swift Playground, XCTest for testing, and much more. Xcode has become an indispensable tool for both novice and experienced developers in the Apple ecosystem.

As we delve deeper into this book, you'll explore the various facets of Xcode and how to leverage its capabilities for successful app development across Apple's platforms.

1.2. Understanding the Xcode Interface

The Xcode interface is the primary workspace where developers create, edit, and manage their projects. Understanding the different components of the Xcode interface is essential for efficient development.

Main Window Layout

When you open Xcode, you'll notice a multi-pane layout that forms the main window. The primary panes include:

- **Navigator Area**: On the left, this area contains the Navigator, which provides access to project files, assets, source control, and more.

- **Editor Area**: In the center, this is where you write and edit your code and design your user interfaces using Interface Builder.

- **Utilities Area**: On the right, this area hosts various inspectors and utilities related to the current file or interface element you're working on.

- **Debug Area**: At the bottom, this area displays debugging information, such as console output and variable values, when debugging your application.

Workspace and Project

Xcode projects contain all the resources and settings needed for an app. Within a project, you can have multiple targets, each representing a different build configuration (e.g., Debug, Release). Projects are organized into workspaces, which can include multiple projects and provide a higher-level structure for managing related codebases.

Source Control Integration

Xcode has built-in support for version control systems like Git. You can access source control features from the Navigator Area, allowing you to commit changes, view commit history, and manage branches directly within the IDE.

Interface Builder Integration

The Editor Area seamlessly integrates Interface Builder, where you design your app's user interfaces visually. You can drag and drop UI elements onto the canvas, create connections between interface elements and code, and customize their properties using the Utilities Area.

Code Editor Features

Xcode's code editor is feature-rich. It offers syntax highlighting, code completion, error checking, and integration with documentation. You can quickly navigate through your code using shortcuts, and the code editor can be customized to suit your preferences.

Debugging and Profiling

Xcode includes powerful debugging and profiling tools. The Debug Area allows you to set breakpoints, inspect variables, and step through your code during execution. Instruments, another tool within Xcode, helps you profile and optimize your app's performance.

Device Simulators

Xcode provides a range of device simulators, allowing you to test your apps on various iOS, macOS, watchOS, and tvOS devices without needing physical hardware. Simulators offer an essential testing environment for different screen sizes, resolutions, and platform features.

Documentation and Help

Accessing documentation and help resources is straightforward in Xcode. The "Quick Help" inspector in the Utilities Area provides context-specific documentation for classes and methods. You can also access Apple's official documentation directly from Xcode to gain insights into APIs and best practices.

Plugins and Extensions

Xcode supports plugins and extensions that enhance its functionality. Developers can install third-party plugins to add features, themes, or integrations that cater to specific development needs.

Understanding the Xcode interface is the first step toward becoming proficient in iOS and macOS app development. As you explore this book, you'll delve deeper into each aspect of Xcode and learn how to harness its power for creating exceptional applications.

1.3. Key Features and Capabilities

Xcode is a comprehensive development environment that offers a wide range of features and capabilities to aid in the creation of macOS, iOS, watchOS, and tvOS applications. Understanding these key features is essential for harnessing the full potential of Xcode.

1.3.1. Integrated Development Environment (IDE)

Xcode provides a complete integrated development environment where developers can write, test, and debug their code within a single application. This tight integration streamlines the development workflow, making it easier to create and manage projects.

1.3.2. Swift and Objective-C Support

Xcode supports both the Swift and Objective-C programming languages, allowing developers to choose the language that best suits their needs. Swift, Apple's modern and powerful language, has become increasingly popular for iOS and macOS development, while Objective-C remains a viable option for legacy projects.

1.3.3. Interface Builder

Interface Builder is a visual design tool integrated into Xcode that enables developers to create user interfaces for their applications without writing code. It simplifies the process of designing app layouts and helps ensure a consistent and visually appealing user experience.

1.3.4. Simulator

Xcode includes a range of simulators that allow developers to test their applications on virtual iOS, macOS, watchOS, and tvOS devices. This is particularly useful for debugging and ensuring that the app functions correctly across various device configurations.

1.3.5. Version Control Integration

Xcode has built-in support for popular version control systems such as Git. Developers can manage their code repositories directly within the IDE, making it easy to collaborate with team members and track changes.

1.3.6. Code Editor and Autocompletion

The Xcode code editor offers features like syntax highlighting, code completion, and inline documentation. These features help developers write code faster and with fewer errors, improving productivity.

1.3.7. Debugging and Profiling Tools

Xcode provides a suite of debugging and profiling tools to help identify and fix issues in your code. This includes breakpoints, a debugger console, and Instruments for performance profiling.

1.3.8. Testing Frameworks

Xcode includes XCTest, Apple's testing framework, which allows developers to write unit tests for their code. Testing is crucial for ensuring the reliability and quality of an application.

1.3.9. Interface Builder Plugins

Developers can create custom Interface Builder plugins to extend its functionality and add new user interface components. This enables the integration of third-party libraries and custom controls seamlessly.

1.3.10. App Distribution and Deployment

Xcode simplifies the process of distributing and deploying applications to the App Store or enterprise environments. It provides tools for code signing, packaging, and submission to the App Store Connect.

1.3.11. Documentation and Help

Access to documentation and help resources is readily available within Xcode. Developers can easily access API documentation, tutorials, and guides to enhance their knowledge and troubleshoot issues.

1.3.12. Asset Management

Xcode includes asset catalogs for managing images, icons, and other assets used in an app. This helps maintain consistency in design and simplifies asset management.

1.3.13. Code Signing and Provisioning

Xcode handles the complexities of code signing and provisioning profiles, ensuring that applications are securely signed and ready for deployment to devices or app stores.

1.3.14. Localization and Internationalization

Developers can internationalize their apps in Xcode, making it easier to reach a global audience. Localization tools assist in adapting the app's user interface to different languages and regions.

Understanding these key features and capabilities of Xcode is essential for any developer embarking on macOS or iOS app development. As you progress through this book, you'll learn how to leverage these tools effectively to create high-quality applications for Apple's platforms.

1.4. Setting Up Your Development Environment

Before you dive into the world of Xcode and app development, it's crucial to set up your development environment properly. A well-configured environment ensures a smooth and productive development process. Here are the key steps to set up your development environment:

1.4.1. Install Xcode

The first step is to install Xcode itself. You can download it for free from the Mac App Store. Xcode includes everything you need to build apps for Apple's platforms, including the code editor, Interface Builder, simulators, and debugging tools.

1.4.2. macOS Version

Ensure that your Mac is running a compatible version of macOS. Xcode's compatibility may vary depending on the Xcode version you plan to use. Check Apple's official documentation for the specific macOS requirements.

1.4.3. Developer Account

You'll need an Apple Developer account to deploy apps to the App Store or test them on physical devices. You can sign up for a free Apple ID, but to access all developer features, consider enrolling in the Apple Developer Program.

1.4.4. Command Line Tools

Xcode includes a set of command-line tools that are essential for development tasks. To install them, open a terminal and run the following command:

xcode-select—install

1.4.5. Git Configuration

If you plan to use Git for version control (which is highly recommended), configure Git with your name and email address:

git config—global user.name "Your Name"

git config—global user.email "your@email.com"

1.4.6. Editor Preferences

Customize the Xcode code editor to match your preferences. You can adjust settings for indentation, code completion, font, and color scheme to make your coding experience comfortable and efficient.

1.4.7. Apple ID and Certificates

For distributing apps, you'll need to create App IDs, provisioning profiles, and signing certificates in your Apple Developer account. Xcode will guide you through these steps, but it's essential to have your Apple Developer account set up.

1.4.8. Testing Devices

If you want to test your apps on physical devices, you'll need to register those devices with your Apple Developer account. Xcode allows you to deploy apps to these devices for testing.

1.4.9. Dependencies and Libraries

If your project requires third-party dependencies or libraries, consider using dependency management tools like CocoaPods or Carthage. These tools simplify the process of integrating external code into your Xcode project.

1.4.10. Continuous Integration

For larger projects or team collaboration, setting up a continuous integration (CI) system can be beneficial. CI tools like Jenkins or Travis CI can automate the building, testing, and deployment of your apps.

1.4.11. Documentation

Familiarize yourself with Apple's official documentation and resources. Xcode provides quick access to this documentation, but it's also available online. Learning to navigate and use the documentation effectively is a valuable skill for developers.

1.4.12. Stay Updated

Regularly check for updates to Xcode and related tools. Apple releases new versions with bug fixes, performance improvements, and new features. Staying up-to-date ensures that you have access to the latest development capabilities.

By following these steps and setting up your development environment correctly, you'll be well-prepared to start your journey into Xcode and app development. A well-configured environment will save you time and frustration as you work on your projects and create amazing apps for Apple's platforms.

1.5. Navigating Through the Documentation

One of the essential skills for any developer is the ability to navigate and make effective use of documentation. In the context of Xcode and app development for Apple's platforms, documentation is a valuable resource that provides information about APIs, frameworks, best practices, and more. Here's how to navigate and utilize documentation effectively:

1.5.1. Integrated Documentation

Xcode includes a built-in documentation viewer that offers quick access to Apple's official documentation. You can access it by selecting "Help" in the menu bar and choosing "Documentation and

API Reference." This opens a documentation browser where you can search for information related to specific topics, classes, methods, or frameworks.

1.5.2. Search Functionality

The documentation browser in Xcode provides a powerful search feature. You can enter keywords, class names, or methods in the search bar to quickly find relevant documentation. As you type, the search results will update dynamically, making it easier to locate the information you need.

1.5.3. Documentation Sets

Xcode organizes documentation into sets, each focused on a specific technology or framework. These sets include:

- **iOS & macOS**: Contains documentation for iOS, macOS, watchOS, and tvOS development.

- **Xcode**: Provides information about Xcode itself, including tips and guides for using the IDE effectively.

- **Swift**: Offers documentation specific to the Swift programming language.

- **Objective-C**: Covers Objective-C language documentation for developers working with legacy code or integrating with older frameworks.

1.5.4. Quick Help Inspector

While writing code in Xcode, you can access quick help for specific classes, methods, or variables by Option-clicking on them. This opens a Quick Help inspector that displays context-specific information about the selected code element, including its documentation, parameters, and return types.

1.5.5. Online Documentation

Apple's official documentation is also available online at the Apple Developer Documentation website. This website is a valuable resource, especially when you need to access documentation outside of Xcode or when collaborating with other developers.

1.5.6. Sample Code and Guides

In addition to API reference documentation, Apple provides sample code and programming guides. These resources can be immensely helpful in understanding how to use specific APIs or frameworks. You can often find sample code projects within Xcode itself or on the Apple Developer website.

1.5.7. Release Notes

Stay informed about changes, updates, and bug fixes by regularly checking release notes. Apple publishes release notes for each new version of its platforms, including iOS, macOS, watchOS, and tvOS. These notes highlight important changes that may impact your development projects.

1.5.8. Stack Overflow and Developer Communities

Developer communities, such as Stack Overflow, are excellent places to seek help and share knowledge. Many experienced developers have faced similar challenges and can offer valuable insights and solutions. When searching for answers online, be sure to validate information from reliable sources.

1.5.9. Personal Notes and Annotations

As you explore documentation, consider making personal notes and annotations. Xcode allows you to add your comments and annotations to documentation pages, which can serve as a valuable reference for your future projects.

Effective navigation through documentation is a skill that can significantly boost your productivity as a developer. Whether you're learning a new framework, troubleshooting an issue, or exploring advanced features, documentation serves as a trusted companion on your journey through Xcode and app development.

Chapter 2: Your First Xcode Project

2.1. Creating a New Project: A Step-by-Step Guide

Creating your first Xcode project is an exciting step towards becoming an app developer. In this section, we'll walk through the process of creating a new project using Xcode, step by step.

2.1.1. Launch Xcode

Start by launching Xcode on your Mac. You can find Xcode in the Applications folder or search for it using Spotlight.

2.1.2. Create a New Project

Once Xcode is open, go to the "File" menu and select "New" > "Project..." You'll be presented with a variety of project templates to choose from, depending on the type of app you want to create. For beginners, the "Single View App" template is a great starting point, as it creates a simple iOS app with a single view.

2.1.3. Configure Your Project

After selecting the project template, click the "Next" button. You'll then need to configure your project by providing some basic information:

- **Product Name**: Enter a name for your app.

- **Team**: If you're enrolled in the Apple Developer Program, select your development team. If not, you can choose "None" for now.

- **Organization Identifier**: This is typically in reverse domain format (e.g., com.example). It ensures your app's bundle identifier is unique.

- **Bundle Identifier**: Xcode will automatically generate a bundle identifier based on your organization identifier and product name.

- **Language**: Choose the programming language you prefer (Swift or Objective-C).

- **User Interface**: Select "Storyboard" for visual interface design.

- **Include Unit Tests**: Enable this option if you want Xcode to create unit test files for your project.

Once you've configured your project settings, click the "Next" button.

2.1.4. Choose a Location

Now, choose a location on your Mac where you want to save your project files. You can leave the default location or specify a custom one. Ensure that the "Create Git repository on my Mac" option is checked if you plan to use version control with Git. Click the "Create" button when you're ready.

2.1.5. Explore the Xcode Interface

Congratulations! You've created your first Xcode project. Take a moment to familiarize yourself with the Xcode interface, as discussed in Chapter 1. You'll see the Navigator Area on the left, the Editor Area in the center, and the Utilities Area on the right.

2.1.6. Design Your User Interface

Since we selected the "Storyboard" option earlier, you can now design your app's user interface using Interface Builder. To do this, open the Main.storyboard file in the project navigator. Here, you can drag and drop UI elements onto the canvas and customize their properties using the Attributes Inspector in the Utilities Area.

2.1.7. Write Your First Code

To add functionality to your app, you'll need to write code. Open the ViewController.swift file in the project navigator. This is where you can write Swift code to control your app's behavior. You can start by implementing functions, connecting UI elements to code (using outlets and actions), and adding your logic.

import UIKit

class ViewController: UIViewController {

override func viewDidLoad() {

super.viewDidLoad()

// Your code goes here

}

// Add your functions and code here

}

2.1.8. Build and Run

To see your app in action, click the "Run" button (a triangular icon) in the Xcode toolbar. Xcode will build your project and launch the iOS Simulator with your app. You can interact with your app as if it were running on a real device.

2.1.9. Debugging

If you encounter issues or want to inspect your code while the app is running, you can set breakpoints by clicking on the left margin in the code editor and then run your app in debug mode. The debugger will pause execution at breakpoints, allowing you to examine variables and step through code.

2.1.10. Stop and Quit

To stop your app in the simulator, press the "Stop" button (a square icon) in the Xcode toolbar. To quit the simulator, simply close its window.

You've now created your first Xcode project and have taken your initial steps into app development. In the upcoming sections of this book, you'll explore more advanced topics, features, and techniques to enhance your app development skills further.

2.2. Understanding Project Structure and Files

When you create a new project in Xcode, it's essential to understand the structure of the project and the purpose of the various files and folders that make up your app's codebase. In this section, we'll explore the typical project structure in Xcode and explain the significance of key files and folders.

2.2.1. Project Navigator

The Project Navigator, located in the leftmost pane of the Xcode interface, is your primary tool for navigating and managing your project's files and resources. It provides a hierarchical view of your project's structure, including folders, source files, assets, and more.

2.2.2. Project Files

- **Main.storyboard**: This file is the main user interface (UI) storyboard for your app. You use Interface Builder to design your app's screens and define the flow of the user interface.

- **AppDelegate.swift**: The AppDelegate is a critical file in your project. It contains the application's entry point and lifecycle methods, allowing you to respond to app events such as launch, backgrounding, and termination.

- **ViewController.swift**: This file represents the initial view controller of your app, connected to the Main.storyboard. It's where you write code to control the behavior of the view and respond to user interactions.

2.2.3. Supporting Files

- **Info.plist**: The Info.plist file contains essential configuration information about your app, including its name, bundle identifier, and permissions. You can edit this file to define app settings and permissions.

- **Assets.xcassets**: This folder is where you manage your app's image and asset resources. It allows you to organize and store images for different device resolutions and platforms.

- **LaunchScreen.storyboard**: The Launch Screen storyboard defines the splash screen that appears when your app launches. It's the first visual impression your users get, and you can customize it using Interface Builder.

- **Main Interface**: This setting in the project settings specifies the storyboard or nib file that serves as the main interface for your app. It's often set to Main.storyboard by default.

- **Product Name**: The product name is the name of your app as it appears on the device's home screen. You can change it in the project settings.

2.2.4. Project Settings

Xcode provides various project settings that you can configure to tailor your app's behavior and appearance. These settings are accessible through the "Project" and "Target" settings tabs. Some common settings include:

- **Deployment Target**: Specifies the minimum iOS or macOS version required to run your app.

- **Device Orientation**: Defines the supported device orientations (portrait, landscape) for your app.

- **App Icons and Launch Images**: Allows you to set custom app icons and launch images for different device sizes and resolutions.

- **Signing & Capabilities**: Configures code signing identities, provisioning profiles, and app capabilities (e.g., push notifications, background modes).

2.2.5. Grouping and Organizing Files

In the Project Navigator, you can create groups and folders to organize your project's files logically. This helps maintain a clear and structured codebase, making it easier to find and manage resources as your project grows.

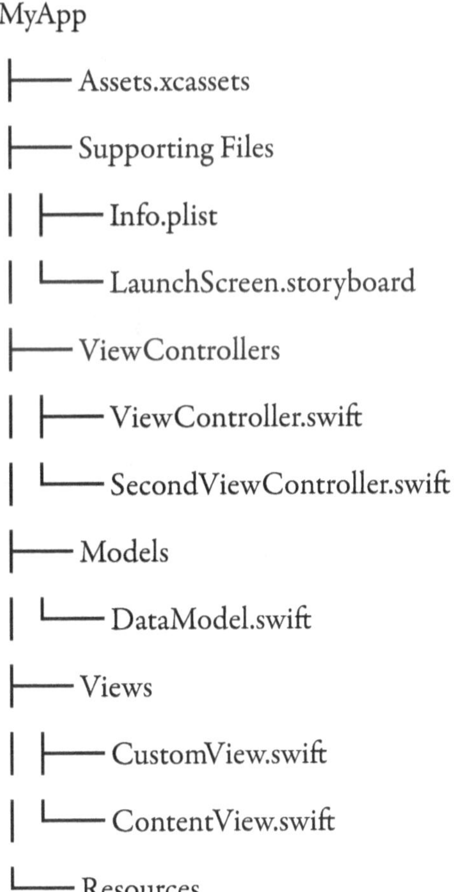

```
MyApp
├── Assets.xcassets
├── Supporting Files
│   ├── Info.plist
│   └── LaunchScreen.storyboard
├── ViewControllers
│   ├── ViewController.swift
│   └── SecondViewController.swift
├── Models
│   └── DataModel.swift
├── Views
│   ├── CustomView.swift
│   └── ContentView.swift
└── Resources
```

```
├──── Images
│   ├──── logo.png
│   └──── icon.png
├──── Sounds
│   └──── alert.mp3
└──── Data
    └──── data.json
```

Understanding your project's structure and the role of each file is crucial for efficient development and collaboration. As you work on your app, you'll create additional files, groups, and resources to implement features, and having a well-organized project will simplify maintenance and debugging.

2.3. Basic Configuration and Settings

Configuring your Xcode project with the right settings is essential to ensure that your app behaves correctly and meets your requirements. In this section, we'll explore some of the basic configuration options and settings you can adjust in Xcode.

2.3.1. Deployment Target

The deployment target specifies the minimum version of the operating system required for your app to run. It's important to choose an appropriate deployment target to ensure your app can reach a wide audience. However, keep in mind that choosing a lower deployment target may limit your access to newer features and APIs.

To set the deployment target:

1. Select your project in the Project Navigator.
2. Choose the target you want to configure.
3. Go to the "General" tab.
4. Under "Deployment Info," select the desired iOS or macOS version from the dropdown menu.

2.3.2. App Icons and Launch Images

App icons and launch images play a crucial role in your app's visual identity. Xcode allows you to customize these assets for different device sizes and resolutions.

App Icons:

1. In the Project Navigator, select the "Assets.xcassets" folder.
2. Inside the asset catalog, you'll find placeholders for app icons. You can drag and drop your app icon images into the appropriate slots, ensuring you provide icons for all required sizes.

Launch Images:

1. The launch screen is defined in the "LaunchScreen.storyboard." You can customize the launch screen using Interface Builder by adding UI elements, images, and text.
2. Make sure your launch screen provides a seamless transition to your app's initial view.

2.3.3. Device Orientation

Controlling the device orientation is important for ensuring your app displays correctly on different devices. You can specify which orientations your app supports and how it should behave when the device rotates.

1. Select your project in the Project Navigator.
2. Choose the target you want to configure.
3. Go to the "General" tab.
4. Under "Deployment Info," check or uncheck the device orientations you want to support.

2.3.4. App Localization

Xcode makes it easy to create multilingual apps. You can add multiple languages and localize your app's user interface, allowing users to experience your app in their preferred language.

1. In the Project Navigator, select your project.
2. Go to the "Info" tab.
3. Click the "+" button under "Localizations" and add the languages you want to support.
4. Xcode will generate localized versions of your storyboard and strings files.

2.3.5. Code Signing and Provisioning Profiles

Code signing ensures that your app's code is trusted and has not been tampered with. Provisioning profiles control how your app can be installed and run on physical devices.

1. Go to the "Signing & Capabilities" tab in your target's settings.
2. Select your development team or create a new one.
3. Xcode will automatically manage provisioning profiles for you.

2.3.6. Custom Build Settings

For advanced configuration, you can customize build settings for your project. These settings allow you to fine-tune your app's behavior and performance.

1. Select your project in the Project Navigator.
2. Choose the target you want to configure.
3. Go to the "Build Settings" tab.
4. Adjust build settings as needed, such as optimization, debugging, and compiler flags.

2.3.7. App Groups and Capabilities

If your app needs to share data between its extensions or with other apps, you can configure App Groups. Additionally, you can enable various app capabilities, such as push notifications, background modes, and iCloud.

1. Go to the "Signing & Capabilities" tab.
2. Enable or configure the required app groups and capabilities.

Understanding and configuring these basic settings is a fundamental aspect of app development in Xcode. Proper configuration ensures your app behaves as expected and provides a smooth user experience across different devices and platforms. As your project progresses, you may need to adjust these settings to accommodate new features or changes in your app's requirements.

2.4. Writing Your First Lines of Code

Now that you have created a new Xcode project, it's time to start writing code to bring your app to life. In this section, we'll guide you through the process of writing your first lines of code using Swift in Xcode.

2.4.1. Understanding ViewController.swift

When you created your Xcode project, a file named "ViewController.swift" was generated. This file represents the initial view controller of your app, connected to the Main.storyboard. It's where you'll write code to control the behavior of the view and respond to user interactions.

2.4.2. ViewDidLoad Method

The viewDidLoad method is one of the fundamental methods in your view controller. It gets called when the view controller's view is loaded into memory. You can override this method to perform any initial setup or configuration for your view.

Here's an example of how the viewDidLoad method looks:

override func viewDidLoad() {

super.viewDidLoad()

// Your code goes here

}

You can add your code inside the curly braces {} to initialize variables, set up the user interface, or perform any other necessary tasks when the view loads.

2.4.3. Adding UI Elements

To interact with the user, you'll typically add UI elements such as buttons, labels, and text fields to your view controller. You can do this either programmatically or using Interface Builder in Main.storyboard.

For example, if you want to add a button programmatically, you can do it like this:

```swift
let myButton = UIButton(type: .system)

myButton.setTitle("Click Me", for: .normal)

myButton.frame = CGRect(x: 100, y: 100, width: 200, height: 40)

myButton.addTarget(self, action: #selector(buttonTapped), for: .touchUpInside)

self.view.addSubview(myButton)
```

This code creates a button, sets its title, frame, and adds it to the view controller's view. It also specifies that the buttonTapped method should be called when the button is tapped.

2.4.4. Responding to User Interactions

To make your app interactive, you'll need to implement methods that respond to user interactions. In the example above, we added a button and specified that the buttonTapped method should be called when the button is tapped.

You can define the buttonTapped method like this:

```swift
@objc func buttonTapped() {

// Handle the button tap here

print("Button tapped!")

}
```

Inside the buttonTapped method, you can write code to perform actions when the button is tapped. In this case, we're simply printing a message to the console.

2.4.5. Connecting UI Elements

When using Interface Builder in Main.storyboard to create your user interface, you can connect UI elements to your code. This is done using "outlets" and "actions."

- An "outlet" is a way to reference a UI element (e.g., a label or a button) in your code. You can change its properties or update its content programmatically.

- An "action" is a method that gets called when a specific UI event occurs (e.g., a button press). You can use actions to respond to user interactions.

To create an outlet or an action:

1. Open Main.storyboard and select the UI element you want to connect.
2. Open the "Assistant Editor" by clicking the "Assistant" button in the Xcode toolbar.
3. Control-drag from the UI element to your code in ViewController.swift.
4. Choose whether you want to create an outlet or an action and provide a name for it.

Once connected, you can access the UI element or respond to events in your code.

@IBOutlet **weak var** myLabel: UILabel!

@IBAction **func** buttonTapped(_ sender: UIButton) {

```
myLabel.text = "Button tapped!"

}
```

In this example, we've created an outlet for a label named myLabel and an action for a button press named buttonTapped. When the button is tapped, the label's text is updated.

With these basics in mind, you can start writing your own code to customize your app's behavior and create interactive user experiences. As you progress in your app development journey, you'll explore more advanced topics and techniques to build robust and feature-rich applications.

2.5. Running and Testing Your Application

Now that you've started writing code for your app, it's crucial to know how to run and test it to ensure it behaves as expected. In this section, we'll explore how to run your app in Xcode's built-in simulator, as well as on physical devices for testing.

2.5.1. Running in the iOS Simulator

Xcode includes an iOS Simulator that allows you to run your app as if it were running on a real iOS device. Here's how to run your app in the simulator:

1. In the Xcode toolbar, select the target device you want to simulate. You can choose from various iPhone and iPad models and versions.
2. Click the "Run" button (a triangular icon) or press Command + R on your keyboard.
3. Xcode will build your project, launch the simulator, and install your app.

4. You'll see your app running in the simulator, and you can interact with it using your mouse and keyboard.
5. To stop the app, click the "Stop" button (a square icon) in the Xcode toolbar.

The simulator is a valuable tool for testing your app's functionality, user interface, and responsiveness on different iOS devices and versions. You can simulate various device orientations and screen sizes to ensure your app looks and works well across the iOS ecosystem.

2.5.2. Running on a Physical Device

Testing your app on a physical iOS device is essential to ensure it performs correctly and to identify any device-specific issues. To run your app on a physical device, follow these steps:

1. Connect your iOS device to your Mac using a USB cable.
2. In the Xcode toolbar, select your connected device as the target.
3. Click the "Run" button (a triangular icon) or press Command + R on your keyboard.
4. Xcode will build your project and install the app on your device.
5. You can now use your iOS device to interact with and test your app.

Running on a physical device provides a more accurate representation of your app's performance, as it takes into account the device's hardware and real-world conditions. It's especially important for testing features like camera access, GPS, and device-specific behaviors.

2.5.3. Debugging Your App

During development, you may encounter issues or unexpected behavior in your app. Xcode provides powerful debugging tools to help you identify and resolve these issues. Here are some debugging features:

- **Breakpoints**: You can set breakpoints in your code by clicking on the left margin in the code editor. When your app reaches a breakpoint, it pauses execution, allowing you to inspect variables and the call stack.

- **Console and LLDB**: The console in Xcode displays log messages and errors generated by your app. You can also interact with the LLDB debugger by entering commands in the console to examine variables and objects.

- **Debug Navigator**: The Debug Navigator provides an overview of your app's performance, including memory usage and CPU usage. It can help you identify performance bottlenecks.

- **View Debugging**: You can inspect the view hierarchy of your app's user interface during runtime, which is useful for diagnosing layout and rendering issues.

- **Instruments**: Instruments is a powerful profiling tool that allows you to analyze your app's performance, memory usage, and energy consumption. It helps you identify and fix performance problems.

Debugging is an integral part of the development process, and Xcode's debugging tools are designed to make it easier to find and fix issues in your code. Learning to use these tools effectively will greatly improve your development workflow.

2.5.4. Testing Your App

In addition to manual testing, Xcode provides a testing framework for writing and running automated tests to ensure your app's functionality remains intact as you make changes or add new features. Testing helps catch regressions and ensures the reliability of your app.

Xcode supports different types of tests, including unit tests, integration tests, and UI tests. You can create test targets within your Xcode project to organize and run tests.

Writing and running tests in Xcode is a comprehensive topic, but here's a brief overview:

- **Unit Tests**: Unit tests focus on testing individual units of code, such as functions or methods, in isolation. They help ensure that each unit of code behaves as expected.

- **Integration Tests**: Integration tests check the interaction between different components or modules of your app. They verify that these components work together correctly.

- **UI Tests**: UI tests simulate user interactions with your app's user interface. They help ensure that the user interface functions correctly and that user flows work as intended.

To create tests, you typically create a separate test file for each component or module you want to test and write test methods that assert expected behaviors. You can then run your tests in Xcode to verify that your app functions correctly.

2.5.5. Performance Tuning with Instruments

For optimizing your app's performance, Xcode provides Instruments, a tool that allows you to profile your app and identify performance bottlenecks. Instruments provides various instruments for measuring CPU usage, memory usage, energy impact, and more.

To use Instruments:

1. Select the "Product" menu in Xcode.
2. Choose "Profile" to launch Instruments.
3. Select a profiling template that matches your performance goals (e.g., Time Profiler, Allocations, Leaks).
4. Start recording your app's performance.
5. Analyze the data to identify areas where your app may be inefficient or consuming excessive resources.
6. Use the insights from Instruments to make improvements to your code and optimize your app's performance.

Performance tuning is an ongoing process, and Instruments is a valuable tool for ensuring that your app runs smoothly and efficiently, even under heavy usage.

By running and testing your app regularly, debugging issues, and optimizing performance, you can ensure that your app provides a high-quality user experience and is ready for deployment to the App Store or distribution to users.

Chapter 3: Interface Builder Unleashed

3.1. Exploring Interface Builder

Interface Builder is a powerful tool within Xcode that allows you to design user interfaces for your iOS or macOS apps visually. In this section, we'll explore the basics of Interface Builder and how to use it to create user interfaces for your projects.

3.1.1. Launching Interface Builder

To access Interface Builder, you'll typically open your Xcode project and select a storyboard or .xib file from the Project Navigator. These files define the layout and design of your app's screens.

1. Open your Xcode project.
2. In the Project Navigator, select a storyboard or .xib file (Interface Builder files).
3. Double-click the selected file to open it in Interface Builder.

3.1.2. Interface Builder Layout

When you open a storyboard or .xib file in Interface Builder, you'll see a visual representation of your app's user interface. Here's an overview of the main components of the Interface Builder interface:

- **Canvas**: The canvas is where you design your user interface by adding and arranging UI elements (e.g., buttons, labels, text fields).

- **Document Outline**: The document outline displays a hierarchical view of all the UI elements in your view controller. You can select and organize elements from here.

• **Object Library**: The object library provides a list of UI elements and components that you can drag and drop onto the canvas. You'll find buttons, labels, text fields, and more here.

• **Inspector**: The inspector panel allows you to configure the properties and attributes of selected UI elements. You can customize appearance, behavior, and other settings here.

3.1.3. Adding UI Elements

To add UI elements to your view controller's scene, follow these steps:

1. Open Interface Builder and ensure your view controller's scene is selected in the canvas.
2. Go to the Object Library (usually located on the right side of the Xcode window).
3. Drag and drop UI elements from the Object Library onto the canvas.
4. Use the Inspector panel to configure the properties and attributes of the selected UI element.
5. Arrange and position the UI elements as desired on the canvas.

3.1.4. Connecting UI Elements

To make your UI elements interactive and responsive, you'll need to connect them to your code. This is done through "outlets" and "actions."

• **Outlets**: Outlets allow you to create references to UI elements in your code, enabling you to access and manipulate them programmatically. To create an outlet, control-drag from the UI element on the canvas to your view controller's Swift file.

• **Actions**: Actions define methods that are called when a specific UI event occurs, such as a button press. To create an action, control-drag from the UI element to your view controller's Swift file and choose the event you want to trigger the action.

3.1.5. Autolayout and Constraints

To ensure your user interface adapts to different device sizes and orientations, you'll use Autolayout and constraints. Constraints define the relationships between UI elements, specifying how they should appear relative to each other and the screen.

1. Select the UI element you want to add constraints to.
2. Click the "Add New Constraints" button in the lower-right corner of the Interface Builder window.
3. Set the constraints based on the desired layout. Common constraints include width, height, leading, trailing, top, and bottom constraints.
4. Interface Builder will automatically update the constraints as you add or move UI elements, ensuring your layout remains consistent.

3.1.6. Preview and Adjustments

Interface Builder offers a real-time preview mode that allows you to see how your user interface looks on different device sizes and orientations without running the app in the simulator. Use the preview buttons in the canvas to switch between device sizes and orientations.

You can also make adjustments directly in the canvas by selecting UI elements and modifying their properties or constraints. The canvas provides a WYSIWYG (What You See Is What You Get) interface for visualizing your design changes.

3.1.7. Interface Builder and Storyboard Segues

Storyboard segues are a powerful way to define navigation and transitions between different view controllers within your app. You can create segues by control-dragging from one view controller to another on the storyboard canvas.

- **Push Segue**: Used for navigation within navigation controllers, typically for drill-down navigation in table views.

- **Modal Segue**: Presents a view controller modally, often used for presenting new screens or forms.

- **Custom Segue**: You can create custom segues with specific animations or transitions between view controllers.

3.1.8. Live Preview and Integration

Interface Builder also offers a Live Preview feature that allows you to see how custom UI components you've built in code will appear in Interface Builder. This can be especially useful when creating custom UI elements and views.

To use Live Preview, define a preview provider in your code that returns a preview of your custom UI component. Interface

3.2. Designing User Interfaces with Storyboards

Storyboards are a visual representation of your app's user interface and the flow of screens or view controllers. They are a fundamental part of iOS and macOS app development, as they allow you to design and organize your app's user interface in a visual and intuitive way. In this section, we'll delve into the process of designing user interfaces using storyboards in Interface Builder.

3.2.1. Creating a New Storyboard

To get started with storyboards, you'll need to create a new one or use an existing one if your project already has one. Here's how to create a new storyboard:

1. Open Xcode and your project.
2. In the Project Navigator, right-click on your project's root folder or an appropriate group within your project.
3. Choose "New File..." from the context menu.
4. In the template chooser, select "Storyboard" under the "User Interface" category.
5. Click "Next," choose a name for your storyboard (e.g., "Main.storyboard" for the main user interface), and click "Create."

3.2.2. Adding View Controllers

In your newly created storyboard, you can start by adding view controllers, which represent individual screens or segments of your app. To add a view controller:

1. Open your storyboard in Interface Builder.
2. Locate the "Object Library" on the right-hand side of the

Xcode window.

3. In the "Object Library," find the "View Controller" object and drag it onto the storyboard canvas.
4. Repeat this process to add as many view controllers as your app requires.
5. To establish relationships between view controllers, you can use segues. Control-drag from one view controller to another to create a segue that defines how navigation occurs between them.

3.2.3. Designing View Controllers

Once you've added view controllers to your storyboard, you can design the user interface for each one by adding UI elements, configuring their properties, and setting up Autolayout constraints to ensure your design adapts to different device sizes.

1. Select a view controller on the storyboard canvas.
2. Use the "Object Library" to drag and drop UI elements onto the view controller's canvas.
3. Configure the properties of each UI element using the "Attributes Inspector" on the right-hand side of Interface Builder.
4. Use Autolayout to define the layout of your UI elements, ensuring they appear correctly on various devices and orientations.

3.2.4. Creating Segues

To define the flow between view controllers in your app, you'll create segues. Segues represent transitions from one view controller to another, such as pushing a view controller onto a navigation stack or presenting a view controller modally.

1. Control-drag from a UI element, such as a button or table view cell, to another view controller on the storyboard canvas.
2. Release the mouse button to bring up a menu. Choose the type of segue you want to create (e.g., "Show," "Present Modally").
3. Configure the segue by selecting it and adjusting its attributes in the "Attributes Inspector."
4. You can also give your segue an identifier, which allows you to trigger it programmatically in your code.

3.2.5. Navigating Between View Controllers

In your code, you can implement navigation and transitions between view controllers by invoking the segues you've created in your storyboard. Here's a basic example of how to perform navigation between view controllers using Swift:

// Swift code to trigger a segue programmatically

performSegue(withIdentifier: "YourSegueIdentifier", sender: **self**)

Replace "YourSegueIdentifier" with the actual identifier of the segue you want to trigger. This code is typically placed in an action method that responds to a user's interaction, such as a button press.

3.2.6. Scene Dock and Navigation Controller

The Scene Dock is a useful tool in Interface Builder for managing view controllers and their relationships. It allows you to organize view controllers within your storyboard and provides a visual representation of the navigation flow.

If your app requires navigation between view controllers, consider using a Navigation Controller. A Navigation Controller manages a stack of view controllers and provides a built-in navigation bar for easy navigation between them. To add a Navigation Controller to your storyboard, drag and drop it from the "Object Library" onto the canvas and set it as the initial view controller if needed.

3.2.7. Previewing User Interfaces

Interface Builder offers a live preview feature that allows you to see how your user interface looks on different devices and orientations without running the app in the simulator. You can choose different device types and screen sizes to preview your design.

To use live preview:

1. Select the view controller or scene you want to preview in the canvas.
2. In the bottom-left corner of Interface Builder, use the preview buttons to select the desired device and orientation.
3. Interface Builder will show a real-time preview of your user interface as it would appear on the selected device.

3.2.8. Custom View Controllers

While view controllers provided by UIKit and AppKit cover most use cases, you can also create custom view controllers to implement unique and complex user interfaces. Custom view controllers allow you to encapsulate specific functionality and design patterns within your app.

To create a custom view controller:

1. Create a new Swift file that subclasses UIViewController or NSViewController for iOS or macOS, respectively.

2. Design your custom user interface within the view controller's view, which can be done in Interface Builder or programmatically in code.
3. Implement any required logic and behaviors within your custom view controller.
4. In your storyboard, drag and drop a "View Controller" from the Object Library onto the canvas.
5. Select the newly added view controller and set its custom class in the "Identity Inspector" to your custom view controller class.

With custom view controllers, you have the flexibility to create tailored user experiences and implement complex features within your app.

3.2.9. Internationalization and Localization

If you plan to release your app in multiple languages, Interface Builder makes it easy to internationalize your user interface. You can create localized versions of your storyboard, strings, and resources to provide a seamless experience for users in different regions.

1. In your storyboard, select the UI elements that contain text to be localized, such as labels and buttons.
2. Open the "Attributes Inspector" and click the "Localization" button.
3. Choose the languages you want to support and specify the localized text for each language.

Xcode will generate language-specific versions of your storyboard files, allowing your app to display the appropriate language based on the user's device settings.

Designing user interfaces with storyboards in Interface Builder is a critical skill for iOS and macOS app developers. It allows you to create visually appealing and user-friendly apps while efficiently managing the navigation flow between view controllers. Whether you're building a simple app or a complex one, storyboards provide a powerful tool for crafting compelling user experiences.

3.3. Connecting UI to Code: Outlets and Actions

In iOS and macOS app development, creating a compelling user interface is only part of the equation. You also need to make your UI elements interactive by connecting them to your Swift code. This is accomplished using outlets and actions. In this section, we'll explore how to establish these connections and enable your app's UI to respond to user interactions.

3.3.1. Outlets: Connecting UI Elements to Code

Outlets are connections that link UI elements defined in your storyboard to properties in your Swift code. By creating outlets, you can access and manipulate UI elements programmatically. Here's how to establish an outlet connection:

1. Open your storyboard in Interface Builder.
2. Select the UI element (e.g., a button or label) that you want to connect to your code.
3. Open the "Identity Inspector" in the right-hand panel.
4. In the "Identity Inspector," find the "Object" section and enter a unique identifier for the UI element in the "Storyboard ID" field. This identifier is used to create an IBOutlet in your code.
5. In your Swift code, declare a property with the @IBOutlet

attribute and specify the type of the UI element (e.g., UILabel, UIButton).

Here's an example of creating an outlet for a UILabel:

@IBOutlet **weak var** titleLabel: UILabel!

In this example, we've created an outlet called titleLabel that links to a UILabel in the storyboard. The weak keyword ensures that the outlet doesn't keep a strong reference to the UI element, preventing memory leaks.

1. To establish the connection between the outlet in your code and the UI element in your storyboard, you can either control-drag from the UI element in Interface Builder to your Swift file or use the "Assistant Editor" to create the connection. Control-dragging creates a visual connection on the storyboard canvas, while the "Assistant Editor" displays the code and allows you to drag from the UI element to the code.

Once the outlet is established, you can access and modify properties of the connected UI element in your Swift code. For instance, you can set the text of a UILabel or enable/disable a UIButton.

3.3.2. Actions: Handling User Interactions

Actions are methods in your Swift code that are triggered by specific UI events, such as button taps or slider adjustments. By creating actions, you can define how your app responds to user interactions with your UI elements. Here's how to establish an action connection:

1. Open your storyboard in Interface Builder.

2. Select the UI element (e.g., a button) for which you want to define an action.
3. Open the "Connections Inspector" in the right-hand panel.
4. In the "Connections Inspector," find the "Sent Events" section.
5. Control-drag from the UI element to your Swift code in the "Assistant Editor."
6. Choose the UI event that should trigger the action (e.g., "Touch Up Inside" for a button press).
7. Provide a name for the action method when prompted. This method will be automatically generated in your Swift code.

Here's an example of creating an action for a UIButton:

```swift
@IBAction func buttonTapped(_ sender: UIButton) {

// Your code to handle the button tap goes here

}
```

In this example, we've defined an action method named buttonTapped that takes a UIButton as a parameter. This method will be called when the button is tapped by the user.

1. Once the action is established, you can implement the desired behavior within the action method. For instance, you can perform calculations, show/hide UI elements, or navigate to another view controller.

3.3.3. Connecting Multiple UI Elements

You can connect multiple UI elements to the same outlet or action, enabling you to perform the same operation on all of them simultaneously. This is useful when you have a group of UI elements that share a similar behavior or appearance.

For example, if you have multiple buttons that should perform the same action, you can connect them to a single action method. Similarly, if you want to update the text of several labels with the same content, you can connect them to a single outlet.

3.3.4. Dynamic UI Elements and Tags

In some cases, you may have a dynamic number of UI elements, such as a variable number of buttons or labels created at runtime. In such situations, you can use tags to identify and manipulate these elements.

1. Assign a unique tag to each dynamic UI element in Interface Builder using the "Attributes Inspector."
2. In your Swift code, you can access these UI elements by their tags using the viewWithTag(_:) method. For example:

if let button = view.viewWithTag(100) **as?** UIButton {

// Access and manipulate the button with tag 100

}

1. Make sure to cast the retrieved view to the appropriate type (e.g., UIButton) before performing any operations.

3.3

3.4. Using Auto Layout for Responsive Designs

Auto Layout is a fundamental concept in iOS and macOS app development that allows you to create user interfaces that adapt gracefully to different screen sizes and orientations. It ensures that your app's UI elements are positioned and sized correctly, regardless of the device it's running on. In this section, we'll explore how to use Auto Layout effectively within Interface Builder to achieve responsive designs.

3.4.1. Introduction to Auto Layout

Auto Layout is a constraint-based system that defines the relationships and rules for the placement and sizing of UI elements within a view. Constraints specify attributes such as the element's position, size, alignment, and spacing relative to other elements or the superview.

Key concepts in Auto Layout include:

- **Constraints**: Rules that describe the layout of UI elements. Constraints are mathematical expressions that define the relationships between attributes, such as width, height, and position.

- **Constraints Hierarchy**: Constraints can be organized hierarchically, with relationships between parent and child views. Constraints can also be applied to a specific element.

- **Intrinsic Content Size**: The natural size of a UI element based on its content, such as the text in a label or the image in an image view.

- **Priority**: Constraints can have priorities that determine how the system resolves conflicts. Higher priority constraints take precedence.

- **Content Compression Resistance and Content Hugging**: These properties control how a UI element resists being compressed or stretched, affecting its size.

- **Autoresizing Masks (iOS only)**: In iOS, autoresizing masks are used in conjunction with Auto Layout to specify how a view resizes when its superview changes size.

3.4.2. Adding and Editing Constraints

To add constraints to your UI elements in Interface Builder:

1. Select the UI element you want to apply constraints to.
2. Click the "Add New Constraints" button in the lower-right corner of the Interface Builder window.
3. In the constraints pop-up, you can specify the desired constraints. Common constraints include width, height, leading, trailing, top, and bottom constraints.
4. Set the values for each constraint as needed, such as constant values for spacing, or relative values to other UI elements.
5. Ensure that the checkboxes for "Constrain to margins" and "Add to margin" are set appropriately based on your design requirements.
6. Click the "Add Constraints" button to apply the constraints to the selected UI element.

You can also edit existing constraints by selecting them from the "Document Outline" or by clicking on the constraints directly in the canvas. Editing constraints allows you to fine-tune your layout to achieve the desired design.

3.4.3. Updating Frames and Constraints

When you apply constraints to UI elements, Interface Builder automatically updates the frames and positions of those elements based on the constraints you've defined. This allows you to create layouts that adapt to different screen sizes and orientations.

To update the frames and constraints for a specific view controller:

1. Select the view controller in Interface Builder.
2. Go to the "Editor" menu and choose "Resolve Auto Layout Issues."
3. From the submenu, you can choose options such as "Update Frames" or "Update Constraints." These actions recalculate and apply the layout based on the constraints.
4. You can also use the "Preview" mode in Interface Builder to see how your layout will appear on different devices and orientations without running the app.

3.4.4. Intrinsic Content Size

Certain UI elements, such as labels and buttons, have intrinsic content size based on their content. Auto Layout takes this intrinsic content size into account when calculating layouts. For example, a label with a long text string will have a larger intrinsic content size than a label with a short string.

You can adjust the constraints to allow UI elements to grow or shrink based on their intrinsic content size by modifying the compression resistance and content hugging priorities. Higher compression resistance means the element resists being made smaller, while higher content hugging means it resists being made larger.

3.4.5. Debugging Auto Layout Issues

Auto Layout issues can sometimes arise, causing unexpected layout problems or constraint conflicts. Xcode provides several tools to help you debug these issues:

- **Auto Layout Debugging**: In Interface Builder, you can enable the "Auto Layout" option in the debug bar to visually see the constraints and possible conflicts in your layout.

- **View Debugging**: In Xcode's "Debug View Hierarchy" tool, you can inspect the view hierarchy of your app and see the frames and constraints applied to each UI element.

- **Console Output**: Xcode may print helpful messages to the console when encountering Auto Layout issues, providing information about which constraints are conflicting.

- **Visual Format Language (VFL) Errors**: If you're using VFL to define constraints in code, Xcode can highlight syntax errors and provide suggestions for corrections.

- **Misplaced Views**: In Interface Builder, the "Misplaced Views" option can help identify UI elements that don't have sufficient constraints to determine their position.

3.4.6. Dynamic Layouts and Size Classes

Size classes in Interface Builder allow you to create adaptive layouts that adjust to different screen sizes and orientations. Size classes categorize devices based on their screen width and height, and you can define different layouts for each size class.

To design layouts for specific size classes:

1. Select a view controller in Interface Builder.
2. Open the "Size Inspector" in the right-hand panel.
3. Use the dropdown menus in the "Size Inspector" to specify the size class you want to customize.
4. Adjust the constraints and UI elements as needed for that size class.
5. Interface Builder will automatically switch between the layouts based on the device's size class.

This feature is particularly useful for creating layouts that work well on both iPhone and iPad or adapting to landscape and portrait orientations.

Auto Layout is a powerful tool for creating responsive and adaptive user interfaces in your iOS and macOS apps. By understanding how to add and edit constraints, work with intrinsic content size, and debug layout issues, you can create layouts that provide a consistent and pleasing user experience across a variety of devices and orientations.

3.5. Customizing UI Elements

Customizing UI elements is a common practice in iOS and macOS app development to give your app a unique look and feel. While Interface Builder provides a range of built-in UI elements, you can further enhance the user experience by customizing their appearance and behavior. In this section, we'll explore various ways to customize UI elements programmatically.

3.5.1. Changing Colors and Styles

One of the simplest ways to customize UI elements is by changing their colors and styles. Most UI elements, such as buttons, labels, and views, have properties that allow you to modify their appearance. For example, you can change the background color of a UIButton or the text color of a UILabel. Here's an example of how to change the background color of a UIButton:

// Swift code to change the background color of a UIButton

```swift
let button = UIButton()

button.backgroundColor = UIColor.blue
```

In this code, we create a UIButton and set its background color to blue. You can choose any color you like to match your app's design.

3.5.2. Custom Fonts and Text Styles

To create a unique typography style for your app, you can customize the fonts and text styles of UI elements. You can specify custom fonts or use system fonts and adjust attributes such as font size, weight, and text alignment. Here's an example of customizing the font of a UILabel:

// Swift code to customize the font of a UILabel

```swift
let label = UILabel()

label.font = UIFont(name: "Helvetica-Bold", size: 18.0)
```

In this code, we create a UILabel and set its font to "Helvetica-Bold" with a font size of 18.0 points. You can replace the font name and size with your preferred choices.

3.5.3. Adding Shadows and Borders

Adding shadows and borders to UI elements can make them stand out and give a sense of depth to your app's interface. You can customize the shadow and border properties of views and buttons. Here's an example of adding a shadow to a UIView:

```swift
// Swift code to add a shadow to a UIView

let view = UIView()

view.layer.shadowColor = UIColor.black.cgColor

view.layer.shadowOpacity = 0.5

view.layer.shadowOffset = CGSize(width: 2.0, height: 2.0)

view.layer.shadowRadius = 5.0
```

In this code, we create a UIView and customize its shadow by setting properties such as shadow color, opacity, offset, and radius. Adjust these values to achieve the desired shadow effect.

3.5.4. Creating Custom UI Elements

While UIKit and AppKit provide a rich set of standard UI elements, you can create entirely custom UI elements when the built-in ones don't meet your requirements. Custom UI elements allow you to design unique interfaces tailored to your app's needs.

To create a custom UI element, you'll typically subclass existing UI classes like UIView or UIControl and override their drawing methods. For example, you can create a custom button by subclassing UIControl and implementing your drawing code in the draw(_:) method. Here's a simplified example:

```swift
// Swift code to create a custom button

class CustomButton: UIControl {

override func draw(_ rect: CGRect) {

// Custom drawing code goes here

let path = UIBezierPath(roundedRect: rect, cornerRadius: 10.0)

UIColor.blue.setFill()

path.fill()

}

}
```

In this code, we create a custom button by subclassing UIControl and overriding the draw(_:) method to draw a rounded rectangle with a blue fill. You can define more complex drawing logic for your custom UI elements.

3.5.5. Adding Gestures and Interactions

Customizing UI elements also involves adding gestures and interactions to make your app more interactive and user-friendly. You can attach gesture recognizers to UI elements to detect user actions such as taps, swipes, and pinches. Then, you can respond to these gestures with custom code.

For example, you can add a UITapGestureRecognizer to a UIImageView to detect when the user taps on an image:

```swift
// Swift code to add a tap gesture recognizer to a UIImageView

let imageView = UIImageView()

let tapGesture = UITapGestureRecognizer(target: self, action:
#selector(imageTapped))

imageView.addGestureRecognizer(tapGesture)

imageView.isUserInteractionEnabled = true // Enable user
interaction
```

In this code, we create a UITapGestureRecognizer and attach it to an UIImageView. When the user taps the image, the imageTapped function will be called.

3.5.6. Animations and Transitions

Customizing UI elements can also involve creating animations and transitions to provide a visually engaging experience. You can animate the appearance, disappearance, and behavior of UI elements to make your app more dynamic. UIKit and AppKit provide animation APIs for these purposes.

For example, you can animate the change in frame of a UIView to create a smooth transition:

```swift
// Swift code to animate a UIView's frame change

UIView.animate(withDuration: 0.5) {

view.frame = CGRect(x: 100, y: 100, width: 200, height: 200)

}
```

In this code, we use the UIView.animate method to animate a UIView's frame change over a duration of 0.5 seconds.

Customizing UI elements is a crucial aspect of creating a distinctive and user-friendly app. By modifying colors, fonts, adding shadows, creating custom elements, and enhancing interactions with gestures and animations, you can tailor your app's UI to align with your design vision and improve the overall user experience. These customization options provide the flexibility needed to craft a polished and engaging interface.

4. Swift Programming in Xcode

4.1. Swift Basics: Syntax and Structure

Swift is a powerful and modern programming language that's used for iOS, macOS, watchOS, and tvOS app development. In this section, we'll dive into the fundamentals of Swift, covering its syntax, structure, and key concepts.

4.1.1. A Brief Introduction to Swift

Swift was introduced by Apple in 2014 as a successor to Objective-C, aiming to provide a more concise, readable, and safe language for app development. It combines features from various programming languages and incorporates modern programming paradigms like functional and object-oriented programming.

Key characteristics of Swift include:

- **Safety**: Swift emphasizes compile-time safety checks to prevent common programming errors. It offers features like optionals and type inference to catch issues early.

- **Performance**: Swift is designed to be fast and efficient. It achieves performance comparable to C and C++ by using a modern LLVM compiler.

- **Expressive Syntax**: Swift features a clean and expressive syntax, making code easier to read and write. It reduces boilerplate code, which can be common in other languages.

- **Interoperability**: Swift is compatible with Objective-C, allowing developers to use both languages within the same project. This facilitates the gradual adoption of Swift in existing codebases.

4.1.2. Hello, World! in Swift

Let's start with the traditional "Hello, World!" program in Swift to get a feel for the language's syntax:

// Swift code for Hello, World!

let greeting = "Hello, World!"

print(greeting)

In this example:

- We declare a constant variable greeting and assign it the string "Hello, World!".

- The print function is used to output the value of greeting to the console.

4.1.3. Variables and Constants

In Swift, you can declare variables and constants using the var and let keywords, respectively. Variables can be modified after declaration, while constants cannot.

var mutableVariable = 42

let constantValue = "This is a constant"

4.1.4. Data Types

Swift provides a range of data types to work with:

- **Integers**: Types like Int and UInt represent signed and unsigned integers, respectively.

- **Floating-Point**: Types like Double and Float represent floating-point numbers.

- **Booleans**: The Bool type represents true or false values.

- **Strings**: The String type represents text.

- **Tuples**: Tuples group multiple values into a single compound value.

- **Arrays**: Arrays are ordered collections of values.

- **Dictionaries**: Dictionaries store key-value pairs.

- **Optionals**: Optionals indicate that a value may be absent (nil).

4.1.5. Control Flow

Swift provides various control flow constructs for making decisions and repeating tasks. These include:

- **Conditional Statements**: if, else, and switch statements for making decisions based on conditions.

- **Loops**: for-in, while, and repeat-while loops for repeating tasks.

4.1.6. Functions

Functions are essential building blocks in Swift. You can define your own functions to encapsulate a set of instructions. Here's a simple function that calculates the square of a number:

```swift
func square(_ number: Int) -> Int {

return number * number

}
```

In this example:

- We define a function called square that takes an integer parameter number.

- The -> Int syntax specifies that the function returns an integer.

- Inside the function, we calculate the square of the input and return the result.

4.1.7. Optionals

Optionals are a unique feature in Swift that allows variables and properties to have a "no value" state. They are indicated by appending a question mark ? to the type. Optionals can either contain a value or be nil.

```swift
var optionalInt: Int? = 42

var anotherOptional: String? = nil
```

Optionals are a key part of Swift's safety mechanisms, helping prevent null pointer errors.

4.1.8. Comments

You can add comments to your Swift code for documentation or explanation. Single-line comments start with //, while multi-line comments are enclosed in /* */.

// This is a single-line comment

*/**

This is a

multi-line comment

**/*

These are the fundamental concepts of Swift's syntax and structure. Swift offers a rich set of features and capabilities for iOS and macOS app development, making it a versatile and powerful language for building a wide range of applications. In the following sections, we'll explore more advanced topics and features of Swift, such as functions, classes, error handling, and advanced Swift features.

4.2. Functions, Classes, and Structures

Functions, classes, and structures are fundamental building blocks in Swift that allow you to define and organize your code in a modular and reusable manner. In this section, we'll explore these concepts in more detail.

4.2.1. Functions

Defining Functions

Functions in Swift are blocks of code that perform a specific task. You can define your own functions to encapsulate a set of instructions. Here's an example of a simple function that adds two integers:

```swift
func add(_ a: Int, _ b: Int) -> Int {

return a + b

}
```

In this example:

- We define a function called add that takes two integer parameters a and b.

- The -> Int syntax specifies that the function returns an integer.

- Inside the function, we calculate the sum of a and b and return the result.

Calling Functions

To call a function, you use its name followed by a pair of parentheses. Here's how you call the add function:

```swift
let result = add(5, 3)

print(result) // Output: 8
```

Function Parameters

Functions can have parameters that allow you to pass values into the function. In the add function above, a and b are parameters. Parameters can have external names (used when calling the function) and internal names (used within the function). In this case, we used _ as an external name to make the function call cleaner.

4.2.2. Classes and Structures

Defining Classes and Structures

Classes and structures are used to define custom data types in Swift. They allow you to create complex objects that have properties and methods. The main difference between classes and structures is that classes are reference types, while structures are value types.

Here's an example of defining a simple class:

```swift
class Person {

var name: String

var age: Int

init(name: String, age: Int) {

self.name = name

self.age = age

}

func sayHello() {

print("Hello, my name is \(name) and I'm \(age) years old.")
```

```
}

}
```

In this example:

- We define a class called Person with two properties: name and age.

- We provide an initializer (init) to set the initial values of the properties.

- We define a method called sayHello that prints a greeting using the name and age properties.

Creating Instances

To create an instance of a class or structure, you use the type's initializer. Here's how you create a Person instance:

let person1 = Person(name: "Alice", age: 30)

let person2 = Person(name: "Bob", age: 25)

person1.sayHello() // *Output: Hello, my name is Alice and I'm 30 years old.*

person2.sayHello() // *Output: Hello, my name is Bob and I'm 25 years old.*

Value vs. Reference Types

As mentioned earlier, classes are reference types, which means that when you assign an instance of a class to a new variable or pass it as a parameter to a function, you're working with a reference to the same instance. Changes made to the instance affect all references to it.

Structures, on the other hand, are value types. When you assign a structure instance to a new variable or pass it as a parameter, you're working with a copy of the original instance. Changes made to the copy do not affect the original instance.

4.2.3. Properties

Properties are variables or constants that are associated with a class, structure, or enumeration. They define characteristics of the instance.

Stored Properties

Stored properties store constant or variable values as part of an instance. Here's an example of a class with stored properties:

```swift
class Rectangle {

var width: Double

var height: Double

init(width: Double, height: Double) {

self.width = width

self.height = height

}

func area() -> Double {

return width * height
```

```
}

}
```

In this example, width and height are stored properties of the Rectangle class.

Computed Properties

Computed properties do not store a value directly. Instead, they provide a getter and an optional setter to retrieve and set the value indirectly. Here's an example of a computed property:

```
class Circle {

var radius: Double

init(radius: Double) {

self.radius = radius

}

var area: Double {

return Double.pi * radius * radius

}

}
```

In this example, area is a computed property that calculates the area of a circle based on its radius.

4.2.4. Methods

Methods are functions that are associated with a class, structure, or enumeration. They define behaviors that instances of these types can perform.

Instance Methods

Instance methods are functions that are called on instances of a class, structure, or enumeration. For example, the sayHello method of the Person class is an instance method.

Type Methods

Type methods are functions that are called on the type itself, rather than on instances of the type. You define type methods using the static keyword. Here's an example of a type method:

```swift
struct Math {

static func square(_ number: Double) -> Double {

return number * number

}

}

let squaredValue = Math.square(5.0) // Calling a type method
```

In this example, square is a type method of the Math structure.

4.2.5. Access Control

Swift provides access control mechanisms to restrict the access level of classes, properties, methods, and other entities in your code. These access control levels include private, fileprivate, internal, and public.

- private: The entity is only accessible within the defining source file.

- fileprivate: The entity is only accessible within the defining file.

- internal: The entity is accessible within the same module (e.g., an app or framework).

- public: The entity is accessible from any source file that imports the module.

You can specify access control levels using the private, fileprivate, internal, or public keywords.

These are the fundamental concepts of functions, classes, and structures in Swift. These building blocks enable you to create organized and reusable code, defining custom types and behavior for your iOS and macOS applications. In the following sections, we'll explore more advanced Swift features and concepts, such as memory management, error handling, and protocol-oriented programming.

4.3. Memory Management and ARC

Memory management is a critical aspect of Swift programming, ensuring that your app efficiently uses system resources and avoids memory leaks. In Swift, memory management is primarily handled by Automatic Reference Counting (ARC). In this section, we'll delve into memory management and how ARC works in Swift.

4.3.1. Automatic Reference Counting (ARC)

ARC is a mechanism in Swift that automatically tracks and manages the allocation and deallocation of memory for class instances. It ensures that memory is released when it is no longer needed, preventing memory leaks and optimizing resource usage. ARC works by keeping track of how many references (or strong references) exist to a particular instance.

4.3.2. Strong References

A strong reference is the most common type of reference in Swift. When you create a new instance of a class and assign it to a variable or constant, that variable or constant holds a strong reference to the instance. As long as there is at least one strong reference to an object, ARC keeps the object alive in memory.

Here's an example of a strong reference:

```swift
class Person {

var name: String

init(name: String) {

self.name = name

}

}

var person1: Person? = Person(name: "Alice")
```

var person2 = person1 *// Both person1 and person2 now reference the same instance*

In this example, person1 and person2 both hold strong references to the same Person instance.

4.3.3. Reference Cycles and Memory Leaks

One common challenge in memory management is the potential for reference cycles, also known as retain cycles. A reference cycle occurs when two or more objects hold strong references to each other, creating a situation where none of them can be deallocated by ARC, leading to a memory leak.

Swift provides several mechanisms to prevent reference cycles:

Weak References

A weak reference is a reference that does not keep a strong hold on the referenced object. Instead, it allows the referenced object to be deallocated if there are no other strong references to it.

class Apartment {

var tenant: Person?

}

class Person {

var name: String

var apartment: Apartment?

init(name: String) {

self.name = name

```
}

}

var person1: Person? = Person(name: "Alice")

var apartment1: Apartment? = Apartment()

person1?.apartment = apartment1

apartment1?.tenant = person1
```

In this example, we use a weak reference for the tenant property in the Apartment class to break the reference cycle.

Unowned References

An unowned reference is similar to a weak reference, but it assumes that the referenced object will never become nil during its lifetime. If you try to access an unowned reference after the referenced object has been deallocated, your app will crash.

```
class Customer {

var creditCard: CreditCard?

}

class CreditCard {

unowned var owner: Customer

init(owner: Customer) {

self.owner = owner

}
```

```
}

var customer1: Customer? = Customer()

var creditCard1: CreditCard? = CreditCard(owner: customer1!)

customer1?.creditCard = creditCard1

creditCard1 = nil // The CreditCard instance may be deallocated, but
owner remains unowned
```

In this example, we use an unowned reference for the owner property in the CreditCard class.

4.3.4. Strong Reference Cycles with Closures

One common scenario where reference cycles can occur is when closures capture self strongly within a class instance. To break such cycles, you can use the [weak self] or [unowned self] capture list in closures.

```
class NetworkManager {

func fetchData(completion: @escaping (Data) -> Void) {

// Simulate fetching data asynchronously

DispatchQueue.global().async { [weak self] in

guard let self = self else { return }

let data = /*... */ // Fetch data from the network

completion(data)

}

}
```

```
}
```

In this example, [weak self] is used to capture a weak reference to self within the closure, avoiding a strong reference cycle.

4.3.5. Deinitialization

In Swift, classes can have a deinitializer, denoted by deinit. A deinitializer is called automatically just before an instance of a class is deallocated. It is a good place to perform cleanup operations, such as releasing resources or closing files.

```swift
class FileHandler {

let file: File

init() {

file = File.open("example.txt")

}

deinit {

file.close()

}

}
```

In this example, the deinit method is used to close the file when the FileHandler instance is deallocated.

4.3.6. Weak and Unowned References in Closures

When using closures with reference types, it's important to consider reference cycles. You should use [weak self] or [unowned self] capture lists when necessary to avoid strong reference cycles.

```swift
class UserManager {

var users: [User] = []

func fetchUsers(completion: @escaping () -> Void) {

// Simulate fetching users asynchronously

DispatchQueue.global().async { [weak self] in

guard let self = self else { return }

self.users = /*...*/ // Fetch users from the network

completion()

}

}

}
```

In this example, [weak self] is used to capture a weak reference to self within the closure, preventing a strong reference cycle.

4.3.7. Conclusion

Memory management is a crucial aspect of iOS and macOS app development, and Automatic Reference Counting (ARC) plays a central role in Swift's memory management strategy. Understanding strong references, weak references, unowned references, and how to break reference cycles is essential for building memory-efficient and leak-free applications. Swift's syntax and features make it easier to handle memory management challenges and ensure your apps run smoothly without excessive memory usage.

4.4. Error Handling in Swift

Error handling is a critical aspect of writing robust and reliable code. Swift provides a robust error-handling model that allows you to handle errors gracefully and propagate them up the call stack when necessary. In this section, we'll explore error handling in Swift and how to work with errors using the try, catch, and throw mechanisms.

4.4.1. Error Types in Swift

In Swift, errors are represented by types that conform to the Error protocol. You can use existing error types provided by Swift or create custom error types by defining your own enums that conform to the Error protocol.

Here's an example of a custom error type:

```swift
enum NetworkError: Error {

case noInternetConnection

case serverError

case authenticationFailed

}
```

In this example, we define a custom error type called NetworkError that can represent various networking-related errors.

4.4.2. Throwing Errors

In Swift, you can throw errors from a function, method, or closure when something goes wrong. To throw an error, use the throw keyword followed by an error instance or an expression that evaluates to an error.

```swift
func divide(_ numerator: Int, by denominator: Int) throws -> Int {

guard denominator != 0 else {

throw NetworkError.divisionByZero

}

return numerator / denominator

}
```

In this example, the divide function throws a NetworkError when attempting to divide by zero.

4.4.3. Handling Errors with do, try, and catch

To handle errors in Swift, you use the do, try, and catch keywords within a do-catch block. Here's the basic structure:

```swift
do {

// Code that can potentially throw an error

let result = try someFunction()

} catch {

// Handle the error here

}
```

In this structure:

- Code that can throw an error is placed within the do block.

- You use the try keyword before calling a function that can potentially throw an error.

- If an error is thrown, the execution flow jumps to the catch block, where you can handle the error.

Here's an example of error handling in action:

```swift
do {

let result = try divide(10, by: 0)

print("Result: \(result)")

} catch NetworkError.divisionByZero {

print("Division by zero error.")

} catch {

print("An error occurred: \(error)")

}
```

In this example, the divide function is called within a do block. Since it throws a NetworkError when attempting to divide by zero, the corresponding catch block for NetworkError.divisionByZero is executed.

4.4.4. Propagating Errors

When you're working with functions that throw errors, you can choose to propagate errors up the call stack by marking your own function as throwing. This allows the calling function to handle the error or propagate it further.

```swift
func processInput(_ input: String) throws -> String {
```

```swift
if input.isEmpty {

throw NetworkError.emptyInput

}

return "Processed: \(input)"

}

func performTask(_ input: String) throws {

let result = try processInput(input)

print(result)

}
```

In this example, the processInput function throws a NetworkError if the input is empty. The performTask function is also marked as throwing, so it can either handle the error or propagate it up the call stack.

4.4.5. Rethrowing Errors

Sometimes, you may want to catch an error within a function and rethrow it for the calling function to handle. You can use the try, catch, and throw keywords to rethrow an error.

```swift
func fetchData() throws -> Data {

// Fetch data from a network source

// ...

}

func processNetworkRequest() throws {
```

```
do {

let data = try fetchData()

// Process the data

} catch {

throw error // Rethrow the error

}

}
```

In this example, the processNetworkRequest function catches any errors thrown by fetchData and then rethrows the same error for the calling function to handle.

4.4.6. Defer Statements

Swift allows you to use the defer keyword to specify code that should be executed regardless of whether an error is thrown or not. defer statements are often used for cleanup tasks, such as closing files or releasing resources.

```
func processData() throws {

let file = openFile()

defer {

closeFile(file) // This will be executed even if an error is thrown

}

// Process the data

// ...
```

```
if errorOccurred {

throw NetworkError.dataProcessingError

}

}
```

In this example, the closeFile function is deferred to ensure that the file is closed, even if an error is thrown during data processing.

4.4.7. Conclusion

Error handling is a crucial aspect of Swift programming that allows you to gracefully handle unexpected situations and failures in your code. By creating custom error types, throwing and catching errors, propagating errors up the call stack, and using defer statements, you can write robust and reliable code that handles errors effectively. Swift's error-handling model provides a powerful mechanism for building resilient applications that can gracefully recover from errors and continue functioning smoothly.

4.5. Advanced Swift Features

Swift is a powerful and versatile programming language that offers a wide range of advanced features and capabilities to help you write clean, efficient, and maintainable code. In this section, we'll explore some of these advanced features, including functional programming, concurrency, advanced type system features, protocol-oriented programming, and the Swift Standard Library.

4.5.1. Functional Programming in Swift

Swift incorporates functional programming concepts that allow you to write code in a functional style. Functional programming promotes the use of functions as first-class citizens, immutability, and the avoidance of side effects. Key features include:

Closures

Closures are self-contained blocks of code that can capture and store references to variables and functions. They can be used for tasks like sorting collections, defining custom operations, and more.

let numbers = [1, 3, 5, 2, 4]

let sortedNumbers = numbers.sorted { $0 < $1 }

In this example, the sorted method takes a closure to define the sorting criteria.

Higher-Order Functions

Swift provides higher-order functions like map, filter, and reduce that allow you to perform operations on collections in a functional way.

let numbers = [1, 2, 3, 4, 5]

let doubled = numbers.map { $0 * 2 }

let evenNumbers = numbers.filter { $0 % 2 == 0 }

let sum = numbers.reduce(0, +)

These functions make it easy to transform and process data in a concise manner.

4.5.2. Concurrency and Parallel Programming

Concurrency is essential for building responsive and efficient applications. Swift provides several concurrency features, including:

Grand Central Dispatch (GCD)

GCD is a low-level API for managing concurrent operations. It allows you to create and manage dispatch queues for executing tasks concurrently.

```swift
let concurrentQueue = DispatchQueue(label: "com.example.concurrent", attributes: .concurrent)

concurrentQueue.async {
    // Code to run concurrently
}
```

GCD simplifies multithreading and helps avoid common concurrency issues.

Async/Await

Introduced in Swift 5.5, async/await is a high-level concurrency model that simplifies asynchronous programming. You can write asynchronous code that looks like synchronous code, making it easier to reason about and debug.

```swift
async {
    let result = await fetchData()
    // Use the fetched data here
```

```
}
```

Async/await improves code readability and maintainability, especially in complex asynchronous scenarios.

4.5.3. Advanced Type System in Swift

Swift's type system is rich and flexible, allowing you to create expressive and safe code. Advanced type features include:

Generics

Generics enable you to write flexible and reusable code by defining functions, structures, and classes that can work with different types.

```swift
func swap<T>(_ a: inout T, _ b: inout T) {

let temp = a

a = b

b = temp

}

var x = 5, y = 10

swap(&x, &y)
```

In this example, swap is a generic function that can swap values of any type.

Associated Types

Associated types in protocols allow you to define placeholder types that conforming types must specify. This is commonly used in protocols like Collection and IteratorProtocol to make them generic.

protocol Stack {

associatedtype Element

mutating func push(_ element: Element)

mutating func pop() -> Element?

}

struct IntStack: Stack {

typealias Element = Int

// *Implementation for IntStack*

}

Here, the Stack protocol has an associated type Element that specifies the type of elements stored in the stack.

4.5.4. Protocol-Oriented Programming

Protocol-oriented programming (POP) is a design paradigm in Swift that emphasizes protocol adoption and composition over inheritance. It encourages the creation of small, reusable protocols that describe behavior. Types can then conform to multiple protocols, allowing for flexible and composable code.

protocol Drawable {

```swift
func draw()

}

protocol Movable {

func move()

}

struct Circle: Drawable, Movable {

func draw() {

// Draw a circle

}

func move() {

// Move the circle

}

}
```

In this example, Circle conforms to both Drawable and Movable protocols, allowing it to have both drawing and moving behavior.

4.5.5. Leveraging Swift's Standard Library

Swift's Standard Library provides a wealth of pre-built data types and algorithms that make common tasks easier. It includes collections like arrays, dictionaries, and sets, as well as utility functions for working with strings, numbers, and dates.

```swift
let numbers = [3, 1, 4, 1, 5, 9]

let sum = numbers.reduce(0, +) // Calculate the sum of elements
```

```swift
let sorted = numbers.sorted() // Sort the array
```

```swift
let maxNumber = numbers.max() // Find the maximum number
```

By leveraging the Standard Library, you can write efficient and reliable code without reinventing the wheel.

4.5.6. Conclusion

Swift's advanced features and capabilities empower developers to write high-quality code that is both efficient and maintainable. Functional programming, concurrency support, an advanced type system, protocol-oriented programming, and the Standard Library are essential tools for iOS and macOS development. By mastering these features, you can build robust and scalable applications that meet the demands of modern software development.

5. Debugging and Error Handling

Debugging is an essential skill for every developer. In this chapter, we will explore various debugging techniques and tools available in Xcode to help you identify and fix issues in your code effectively. We will also delve into error handling, which is crucial for handling unexpected situations and preventing crashes in your applications.

5.1. Introduction to Debugging in Xcode

Debugging is the process of identifying and fixing issues, bugs, and errors in your code. Xcode provides a powerful set of tools and features to assist you in this process. In this section, we'll introduce you to the fundamentals of debugging in Xcode.

5.1.1. Breakpoints and Step-by-Step Execution

One of the most fundamental debugging tools in Xcode is breakpoints. A breakpoint is a marker you place in your code to pause the execution of your program at a specific line or function. This allows you to inspect the program's state, variables, and behavior at that point.

To set a breakpoint, simply click on the line number in the code editor's gutter. When your app reaches the breakpoint during execution, it will pause, and Xcode will provide you with a variety of debugging options.

You can use the following basic controls for stepping through your code:

- **Step Over**: Continue to the next line of code in the current function.

- **Step Into**: If the current line contains a function call, move into that function and pause at the first line inside the function.

- **Step Out**: If you're inside a function, step out of the current function and pause at the line after the function call in the calling function.

- **Continue**: Resume normal execution until the next breakpoint is encountered.

These controls help you navigate through your code step by step, making it easier to pinpoint the source of issues.

5.1.2. Analyzing Runtime Errors and Crashes

Xcode provides robust tools for diagnosing runtime errors and crashes in your application. When your app crashes, Xcode can provide you with a detailed crash report, including the stack trace, which indicates the sequence of function calls leading up to the crash.

To examine a crash report, go to the "Debug Navigator" and look for the "Debug Session" section. Here, you can see the stack trace, variables, and the exact line of code where the crash occurred. This information is invaluable for identifying the root cause of the issue.

5.1.3. Using the Console and LLDB

The console is a vital tool for debugging in Xcode. You can print messages and variable values to the console using the print function or by adding breakpoints with "Log" actions. This allows you to inspect the values of variables and understand the flow of your program.

Additionally, Xcode integrates with LLDB (Low-Level Debugger), a powerful command-line debugger. You can open the LLDB console by selecting "Debug > Debug Workflow > Show Debug Console" or by clicking the LLDB icon in the debug area. LLDB enables you to execute debugger commands, inspect variables, and manipulate your program during debugging.

5.1.4. Performance Tuning with Instruments

Instruments is a profiling and performance analysis tool that comes bundled with Xcode. It helps you identify performance bottlenecks, memory issues, and other problems in your app. You can use Instruments to run specific tests and gather data on CPU usage, memory usage, disk I/O, and more.

To use Instruments, select "Product > Profile" from the Xcode menu. Then, choose the instrument you want to use, such as the "Time Profiler" or "Allocations" instrument. Instruments will provide detailed information about your app's behavior, allowing you to optimize performance and eliminate memory leaks.

5.1.5. Conclusion

Effective debugging is an essential skill for software developers, and Xcode provides a comprehensive set of tools to make the process easier and more efficient. In this section, we introduced you to the basics of debugging in Xcode, including setting breakpoints, stepping through code, analyzing crashes, using the console and LLDB, and leveraging the power of Instruments for performance tuning. Debugging is a fundamental part of the development process, and mastering these tools will help you become a more proficient and efficient developer.

5.2. Breakpoints and Step-by-Step Execution

In the world of debugging, breakpoints are your best friends. They allow you to pause the execution of your code at a specific point and inspect its state. Xcode provides a powerful set of breakpoint features that go beyond just stopping the program flow. In this section, we'll dive deeper into breakpoints and step-by-step execution.

5.2.1. Types of Breakpoints

Xcode offers several types of breakpoints to cater to different debugging scenarios:

- **Symbolic Breakpoints**: These breakpoints trigger when a specific function or method is called, and you can specify conditions for them.

- **Exception Breakpoints**: They stop execution when exceptions like Swift errors or Objective-C exceptions are thrown.

- **Log Breakpoints**: Log breakpoints don't pause execution but print a message to the console when hit.

- **Conditional Breakpoints**: You can set conditions for breakpoints to trigger only when certain conditions are met.

- **Debugger Command Breakpoints**: These allow you to run custom LLDB debugger commands when the breakpoint is hit.

To add a breakpoint, click on the gutter to the left of your code, or use the shortcut Cmd+\. You can also right-click on an existing breakpoint to edit its properties.

5.2.2. Actions and Conditions

Breakpoints in Xcode can do more than just pause your program. You can attach actions to breakpoints to perform various tasks, such as logging values, running scripts, or even continuing execution after hitting the breakpoint. Actions are defined in the breakpoint's settings, and you can have multiple actions for a single breakpoint.

Conditions, on the other hand, allow you to specify when a breakpoint should be triggered. You can set conditions based on variables, expressions, or other contextual information. This is extremely useful when you only want the breakpoint to trigger under certain circumstances.

5.2.3. Debugging with Step Controls

Once your code hits a breakpoint, you can use the step controls to navigate through your code:

- **Step Over (F6):** This moves to the next line of code in the current function without diving into function calls. If the current line contains a function call, it will execute the function and return control to the caller.

- **Step Into (F7):** Use this to dive into a function or method. If the current line contains a function call, it will take you into that function's code.

- **Step Out (F8)**: When you're inside a function, this allows you to exit the current function and return to the calling function.

- **Continue (F5)**: This resumes normal execution until the next breakpoint or exception.

These step controls are invaluable for understanding how your code flows and for tracking down the source of issues.

5.2.4. Debugging Threads and Queues

In multi-threaded or concurrent code, it's essential to debug each thread separately. Xcode allows you to switch between threads and even provides a visual representation of thread activity in the debugger navigator. This is incredibly useful for identifying race conditions and deadlocks.

Additionally, if you're dealing with code that uses Grand Central Dispatch (GCD) or other asynchronous patterns, you can use the "Queue" view in the debugger to inspect the state of dispatch queues and track asynchronous execution.

5.2.5. Debugging Tips

Here are some additional tips for effective debugging in Xcode:

- Use "Add Exception Breakpoint" (from the "+" button in the breakpoints navigator) to quickly catch and diagnose exceptions in your code.

- Utilize the "Variable View" and "Quick Look" features to inspect the values of variables and expressions.

• Use "Edit Breakpoint" (right-click on a breakpoint) to set conditions and actions specific to your debugging needs.

• Mastering LLDB commands can be a significant asset. You can use them in the LLDB console to inspect and manipulate your program during debugging.

5.2.6. Conclusion

Breakpoints and step-by-step execution are fundamental tools for debugging in Xcode. Understanding the different types of breakpoints, attaching actions and conditions, and effectively using the step controls will significantly improve your ability to diagnose and fix issues in your code. With practice, you'll become a proficient debugger, capable of unraveling complex problems and building more reliable software.

5.3. Analyzing Runtime Errors and Crashes

Runtime errors and crashes can be frustrating to deal with, but they are an inevitable part of software development. In this section, we will explore how to effectively analyze and diagnose runtime errors and crashes using Xcode's debugging tools.

5.3.1. The Importance of Crash Reports

When your app crashes during runtime, it generates a crash report that contains valuable information about the crash, including the stack trace, the sequence of function calls that led to the crash, and the line of code where it occurred. This information is crucial for identifying and fixing the underlying issue.

Xcode makes it easy to access crash reports. If your app crashes while running in Xcode's debugger, you'll see the crash report in the debug navigator. You can also find crash reports in the "Reports" section of the "Devices and Simulators" window.

5.3.2. Understanding the Stack Trace

The stack trace is one of the most important parts of a crash report. It provides a detailed list of the functions and methods that were called leading up to the crash. Each entry in the stack trace represents a point in the code where a function was called.

By examining the stack trace, you can trace the execution flow of your code and identify the specific function or method that caused the crash. Look for the function at the top of the stack trace (the most recent call) and work your way down to find the root cause.

5.3.3. Symbolicating Crash Reports

When you view a crash report in Xcode, you may notice that some parts of the stack trace appear as memory addresses rather than function or method names. This happens because crash reports are initially generated with symbolic information stripped to save space. To make sense of these memory addresses, you need to symbolicate the crash report.

Symbolicating a crash report involves translating memory addresses back into human-readable function and method names. Xcode can automatically symbolicate crash reports for you. When you open a crash report in the "Devices and Simulators" window, Xcode will attempt to download the necessary symbol files from the App Store Connect or your development team.

5.3.4. Analyzing Crash Reports

Once you have a symbolicated crash report, you can start analyzing it to pinpoint the cause of the crash. Here are some tips for effective crash analysis:

- **Identify the Exception**: Look for any exception information in the crash report. The exception type and reason can provide valuable clues about what went wrong.

- **Examine the Stack Trace**: Carefully review the stack trace to find the function or method that triggered the crash. Pay attention to any custom code you wrote in that function.

- **Check for Null or Uninitialized Pointers**: Crashes often occur when you try to access or modify a null or uninitialized pointer. Look for lines of code that involve pointer operations.

- **Review Memory-Related Issues**: Memory-related issues like accessing deallocated objects or dereferencing invalid memory addresses can lead to crashes. Inspect memory-related calls in the stack trace.

- **Look for Thread Information**: If the crash occurred on a background thread or during a concurrent operation, check the thread information in the crash report to understand the context of the crash.

5.3.5. Reproducing the Issue

Analyzing a crash report is only the first step. To fix the issue, you need to reproduce it consistently. This involves understanding the circumstances and conditions under which the crash occurs. Once you can reproduce the issue reliably, you can use breakpoints and debugging techniques to narrow down the problem and make the necessary fixes.

5.3.6. Preventing Future Crashes

After identifying and fixing the cause of a crash, it's essential to test your app thoroughly to ensure that the issue has been resolved. Additionally, consider implementing error-handling mechanisms and defensive programming practices to catch and handle potential issues before they lead to crashes.

Runtime errors and crashes are challenging but manageable aspects of software development. With the right debugging tools and practices, you can diagnose and fix issues effectively, improving the stability and reliability of your applications.

5.4. Using the Console and LLDB

The console is a crucial tool for debugging in Xcode. It allows you to print messages and variable values, helping you gain insights into the state of your application during runtime. In this section, we will explore how to use the console effectively for debugging, and we will introduce LLDB (Low-Level Debugger), Xcode's powerful command-line debugging tool.

5.4.1. Printing Messages and Variables

Printing messages and variable values to the console is one of the simplest yet most effective ways to understand what's happening in your code. You can use the print function in Swift to output text and variable values to the console.

For example, to print a message, you can use:

print("Debugging message")

To print the value of a variable, you can include it in the print statement:

let number = 42

print("The value of 'number' is \(number)")

These print statements will display their output in the console, providing you with valuable information about the flow of your program and the values of variables at specific points in your code.

5.4.2. Logging with Breakpoints

While manually adding print statements is useful, Xcode offers a more powerful way to log information during debugging—log breakpoints. You can create breakpoints with "Log" actions, which will automatically log messages or variable values when the breakpoint is hit.

To create a log breakpoint, follow these steps:

1. Set a breakpoint by clicking in the gutter next to a line of code.
2. Right-click on the breakpoint in the breakpoints navigator and choose "Edit Breakpoint."
3. In the breakpoint settings, add a "Log" action and specify the message or variable value you want to log.

When the breakpoint is hit during debugging, Xcode will log the specified information to the console. This allows you to capture specific data without cluttering your code with excessive print statements.

5.4.3. LLDB (Low-Level Debugger)

LLDB is a command-line debugger that comes integrated with Xcode. It offers advanced debugging capabilities and can be a valuable tool for diagnosing complex issues. You can access the LLDB console in Xcode by selecting "Debug > Debug Workflow > Show Debug Console" or by clicking the LLDB icon in the debug area.

With LLDB, you can execute debugger commands, inspect variables, and manipulate your program during debugging. Some common LLDB commands include:

- po: Short for "print object," this command allows you to inspect the value of variables and expressions.

- bt: This command displays the backtrace, showing the sequence of function calls leading up to the current point in the program.

- c: Short for "continue," this command resumes program execution until the next breakpoint or exception is encountered.

- e: Use this command to evaluate expressions during debugging.

LLDB can be a powerful tool for debugging complex issues or for automating debugging tasks through scripts. Learning the basics of LLDB commands can significantly enhance your debugging skills.

5.4.4. Logging Levels and Filtering

Xcode allows you to control the verbosity of logs by setting different logging levels. By default, logs are displayed with the "All" level, but you can change this level to filter out less important log messages.

To change the logging level, use the drop-down menu in the console. You can select from various levels like "All," "Errors and Warnings," "Errors Only," or "None." Adjusting the logging level can help you focus on the most critical information during debugging.

5.4.5. Custom Formatting

If you prefer a specific format for your log messages, you can customize the log format in Xcode. By going to "Xcode > Preferences > Behaviors," you can modify the format of log messages to suit your preferences. Custom formatting can make your log messages more informative and easier to read.

5.4.6. Conclusion

The console and LLDB are essential tools for effective debugging in Xcode. By using print statements, log breakpoints, and LLDB commands, you can gain insights into your code's behavior, inspect variable values, and diagnose issues. Customizing log levels and formats can further enhance your debugging experience. Mastering these debugging techniques will make you a more proficient and efficient developer, capable of tackling complex problems with confidence.

5.5. Performance Tuning with Instruments

Optimizing the performance of your iOS or macOS application is crucial to providing a smooth and responsive user experience. In this section, we'll explore how you can use Instruments, a profiling and performance analysis tool in Xcode, to identify bottlenecks, memory issues, and other performance problems in your app.

5.5.1. Introduction to Instruments

Instruments is a powerful tool that allows you to collect data on various aspects of your application's performance. It can help you detect issues related to CPU usage, memory consumption, disk I/O, and more. Instruments provides a range of built-in instruments, and you can create custom instruments to gather specific data relevant to your app.

To launch Instruments from Xcode, select "Product > Profile" from the menu. You can choose from a list of available instruments or create a custom instrument configuration. Once your app is running in Instruments, you can start recording performance data.

5.5.2. Time Profiler

The "Time Profiler" instrument is one of the most commonly used instruments for identifying CPU-related performance issues. It provides a visual representation of your app's call stack and shows you which functions are consuming the most CPU time.

When you run the "Time Profiler" instrument, it samples your app's call stack at regular intervals, giving you a snapshot of where the CPU time is being spent. By analyzing the call tree, you can pinpoint functions or methods that are taking up excessive CPU time and causing performance bottlenecks.

5.5.3. Allocations

The "Allocations" instrument is essential for tracking memory usage in your app. It shows you the memory allocation and deallocation patterns, helping you identify memory leaks and inefficient memory management.

When you run the "Allocations" instrument, it tracks memory allocations, releases, and retains over time. You can view a list of allocated memory objects and analyze their memory usage. By identifying objects that are not being deallocated properly, you can address memory leaks and reduce memory overhead.

5.5.4. Leaks

The "Leaks" instrument is dedicated to finding memory leaks in your application. Memory leaks occur when objects are allocated but not deallocated when they are no longer needed. These leaks can lead to increased memory consumption and eventual app crashes.

When you run the "Leaks" instrument, it analyzes your app's memory usage and reports any memory leaks it detects. It provides information about the type of object that leaked, its size, and where it was allocated in your code. By fixing memory leaks, you can improve your app's stability and performance.

5.5.5. Other Instruments

In addition to "Time Profiler," "Allocations," and "Leaks," Instruments offers a wide range of other instruments for performance tuning. Some of these instruments include:

- **Energy Impact**: Measures the energy consumption of your app and helps optimize it for longer battery life.

- **Core Data**: Analyzes the performance of Core Data operations and database queries.

- **File Activity**: Monitors file I/O operations and helps identify performance bottlenecks related to disk access.

- **Network**: Tracks network activity, including network requests and responses, to optimize networking performance.

5.5.6. Analyzing Performance Data

Once you've collected performance data using Instruments, it's crucial to analyze the results. Look for patterns and outliers in the data. Identify areas of your code where CPU usage or memory consumption is unexpectedly high. Pay attention to functions or methods that appear frequently in the call stack.

After identifying performance issues, you can take steps to optimize your code. This may involve refactoring code to make it more efficient, reducing memory usage, or implementing asynchronous operations to improve responsiveness.

5.5.7. Conclusion

Performance tuning with Instruments is an essential part of iOS and macOS app development. By using Instruments to profile your app's performance, you can identify and address performance bottlenecks, memory issues, and other performance-related problems. This leads to a more responsive and efficient application, enhancing the user experience and ensuring your app runs smoothly on a variety of devices.

Chapter 6: Version Control Integration

6.1. Integrating Git with Xcode

Version control is an essential part of software development, allowing developers to track changes, collaborate effectively, and manage codebases efficiently. In this section, we'll explore how to integrate Git with Xcode, one of the most popular version control systems.

Setting Up Git in Xcode

Before you can start using Git in Xcode, you need to make sure that Git is installed on your system. If it's not already installed, you can download and install it from the official Git website or use a package manager like Homebrew on macOS.

Once Git is installed, follow these steps to configure it in Xcode:

1. Open Xcode and go to the "Xcode" menu.
2. Select "Preferences."
3. In the Preferences window, go to the "Source Control" tab.
4. Under "Git Configuration," make sure the path to the Git executable is correctly set. Xcode should automatically detect the Git path if it's installed in the standard location.

Creating a New Git Repository

Now that Git is configured, you can create a new Git repository for your Xcode project. Follow these steps to initiate version control for your project:

1. Open your Xcode project.

2. In the Xcode menu, go to "Source Control" and select "Create Git Repositories..."
3. Choose the location for your Git repository. By default, Xcode suggests creating it in the same directory as your project.

Xcode will initialize a Git repository for your project, and you'll see the Source Control navigator in the left sidebar. This navigator provides you with Git-related functionalities, including status, commits, branches, and more.

Staging and Committing Changes

Once your project is under version control, you can start making changes and tracking them with Git. Here's how you stage and commit changes in Xcode:

1. Make changes to your project's files.
2. Open the Source Control navigator.
3. In the "Uncommitted Changes" section, you'll see a list of the files with changes. Select the files you want to commit by checking the checkboxes next to them.
4. Enter a commit message in the text field below the file list.
5. Click the "Commit" button.

Your changes are now committed to the Git repository. You can also use the "Commit" menu item to commit your changes quickly.

Branching and Merging

Git allows you to work on different branches of your project concurrently. This is particularly useful for developing new features or fixing bugs without affecting the main codebase. Here's how you can create and switch between branches in Xcode:

1. In the Source Control navigator, click on the "Branches" section.
2. Click the "+" button to create a new branch.
3. Enter a name for your new branch and select the base branch.
4. Click "Create."

You can now switch between branches using the Source Control navigator, making it easy to work on different aspects of your project simultaneously.

Viewing Git History

Xcode provides a convenient way to view the Git history of your project. In the Source Control navigator, you can see a list of commits with commit messages and timestamps. Clicking on a commit allows you to see the changes made in that commit, making it easier to track the progress of your project.

In conclusion, integrating Git with Xcode is essential for efficient version control and collaboration in iOS and macOS app development. It allows you to track changes, work on different branches, and collaborate with team members effectively. This section has provided an overview of how to set up and use Git within Xcode, helping you get started with version control in your projects.

6.2. Managing Branches and Merges

Branch management is a critical aspect of using Git effectively in your Xcode projects. Branches allow you to work on different features, bug fixes, or experiments independently without affecting the main codebase. In this section, we'll delve into managing branches and performing merges in Xcode.

Creating a New Branch

Creating a new branch is a common operation in Git, and Xcode provides a straightforward way to do it. Here's how you can create a new branch for your project:

1. Open your Xcode project.
2. Go to the Source Control navigator in the left sidebar.
3. Click on the "Branches" section to reveal the list of existing branches.
4. At the bottom of the branches list, click the "+" button to create a new branch.
5. Enter a name for your new branch and choose the base branch from which you want to create it.
6. Click "Create Branch."

Xcode will create the new branch, and you'll automatically switch to it. Now you can work on this branch independently, making changes specific to your feature or bug fix.

Switching Between Branches

Switching between branches is as simple as selecting the branch you want to work on in the Source Control navigator. Xcode will automatically update your working directory to reflect the selected branch's state.

To switch between branches:

1. Open your Xcode project.
2. Go to the Source Control navigator.
3. In the "Branches" section, click on the branch you want to switch to.

Your working directory will be updated to match the selected branch, allowing you to continue your work seamlessly.

Merging Branches

Merging is the process of combining changes from one branch into another. This is typically done when you've completed work on a feature branch and want to incorporate those changes into the main branch (often called "master" or "main").

Here's how you can merge changes from one branch into another using Xcode:

1. Open your Xcode project.
2. Go to the Source Control navigator.
3. Click on the branch you want to merge changes into (the target branch).
4. Click the "Merge" button in the toolbar.

Xcode will prompt you to select the source branch that contains the changes you want to merge. Choose the source branch and confirm the merge. Xcode will automatically perform the merge operation and resolve any conflicts if they arise.

Resolving Conflicts

Conflicts can occur during a merge when the changes in the source branch and the target branch overlap or conflict with each other. Xcode provides tools to help you resolve these conflicts.

When a conflict occurs, Xcode will display markers in the affected files, indicating the conflicting sections. You can then open the file, review the conflicting changes, and manually choose which changes to keep.

After resolving conflicts, you need to commit the changes to finalize the merge. Xcode will automatically create a merge commit with both branches' changes.

Deleting Branches

Once you've completed work on a branch and merged its changes into the main branch, you may want to delete the feature branch to keep your repository clean. To delete a branch in Xcode:

1. Open your Xcode project.
2. Go to the Source Control navigator.
3. In the "Branches" section, right-click on the branch you want to delete.
4. Select "Delete ."

Xcode will confirm the deletion, and the branch will be removed from your repository.

In summary, managing branches and performing merges are essential skills when using Git in Xcode. Branches allow you to work on different aspects of your project independently, and merging helps you incorporate changes seamlessly. Xcode's integration with Git simplifies these operations, making version control a powerful tool for collaborative iOS and macOS app development.

6.3. Resolving Conflicts

Conflicts are an inevitable part of collaborative software development when using version control systems like Git. Conflicts occur when two or more developers make changes to the same part of a file, and Git cannot automatically determine which changes should take precedence. In this section, we'll explore how to resolve conflicts effectively in Xcode.

Understanding Conflict Markers

When a conflict arises, Git marks the conflicting sections within the affected files with special markers. These markers help you identify and resolve the conflicting changes. The conflict markers typically look like this:

<<<<<<< HEAD

// Your changes

=======

// Incoming changes

>>>>>>> branch-name

- <<<<<<< HEAD: This marker indicates the beginning of the changes made in your current branch (the branch you are merging into).

- =======: Separates the changes made in your branch from the incoming changes (changes from the branch you are merging).

- >>>>>>> branch-name: Marks the end of the incoming changes from the specified branch.

Resolving Conflicts in Xcode

Xcode provides a user-friendly interface for resolving conflicts. Here's a step-by-step guide on how to resolve conflicts using Xcode:

1. Open your Xcode project.
2. Navigate to the Source Control navigator in the left sidebar.
3. Under the "Uncommitted Changes" section, you'll see a list of files with conflicts. These files will have a badge indicating the number of conflicts.
4. Click on the conflicted file to open it in the code editor.
5. In the code editor, you will see the conflict markers indicating the conflicting sections.

```
<<<<<<< HEAD

// Your changes

=======

// Incoming changes

>>>>>>> branch-name
```

1. Manually review and edit the code to resolve the conflict. Decide which changes to keep and which to discard.

Remove the conflict markers and adjust the code accordingly.

// Your resolved code

1. After resolving the conflict, save the file.

Marking Conflicts as Resolved

Xcode provides a convenient way to mark conflicts as resolved after you've edited the code. Here's how to do it:

1. In the Source Control navigator, select the file that you've resolved the conflicts in.
2. Right-click on the file and choose "Mark as Resolved."
3. Xcode will confirm that the conflicts have been marked as resolved.

Committing the Resolved Changes

Once you've resolved all conflicts in your project, you need to commit the changes to finalize the merge. Follow these steps:

1. In the Source Control navigator, select the files that you've resolved conflicts in.
2. Enter a commit message describing the conflict resolution.
3. Click the "Commit" button.

Xcode will create a commit that includes the resolved changes, and the conflicts will be officially resolved in your branch.

Testing the Merge

After resolving conflicts and committing the changes, it's essential to test your code thoroughly. Ensure that the merged changes work as expected and have not introduced new issues. Running your unit tests and conducting manual testing can help verify the integrity of the merged code.

In summary, resolving conflicts is a crucial part of collaborative development, and Xcode provides a straightforward interface for managing conflicts when working with Git. By understanding conflict markers, manually resolving conflicts, marking them as resolved, and committing the changes, you can effectively address conflicts and maintain a smooth workflow in your Xcode projects.

6.4. Best Practices for Version Control

Effective version control is essential for maintaining a stable and collaborative development environment in Xcode. In this section, we'll discuss best practices and strategies for using version control in your iOS and macOS projects.

1. Use Descriptive Branch Names

When creating branches for your Xcode project, use descriptive names that reflect the purpose of the branch. A clear branch naming convention makes it easier for you and your team to understand the context of each branch. For example, use names like "feature/user-authentication" or "bugfix/issue-123" instead of generic names like "branch1" or "new-feature."

2. Frequent Commits

Make frequent and granular commits as you work on your project. Each commit should represent a logical and incremental step in your development process. This practice helps in tracking changes, reviewing history, and isolating issues if they arise.

3. Commit Before Pulling

Before pulling changes from the remote repository (e.g., GitHub, GitLab, Bitbucket), ensure that your local branch is clean and does not have uncommitted changes. Commit or stash your changes to avoid potential conflicts during the pull operation.

4. Regular Pulls and Updates

Frequently pull changes from the remote repository to keep your local branch up to date with the latest developments from your team. Regularly updating your branch reduces the chances of conflicts and integration issues down the line.

5. Branch Cleanup

Delete feature branches after they have been merged into the main branch. Keeping your repository free of unnecessary branches helps maintain a tidy and organized project history.

6. Review Changes Before Committing

Before committing your changes, review the modifications you've made. Verify that your code is clean, adheres to coding standards, and functions as expected. This helps prevent unnecessary bugs and makes code reviews more manageable.

7. Write Meaningful Commit Messages

Write clear and informative commit messages that describe the purpose and impact of the changes. A well-written commit message is invaluable for understanding the history of your project and for tracking down specific changes when needed.

8. Use Git Ignore

Create and maintain a .gitignore file in your project's root directory to specify files and directories that should be excluded from version control. This ensures that generated files, build artifacts, and sensitive information are not accidentally committed to the repository.

9. Embrace Code Reviews

Collaborative code reviews are an integral part of the development process. Encourage team members to review each other's code before merging it into the main branch. Code reviews help catch issues early and ensure code quality.

10. Backup and Restore

Regularly back up your Xcode project and repository to prevent data loss. Familiarize yourself with Git's backup and restore capabilities, such as creating tags or branches for specific project milestones.

11. Documentation

Document your project's structure, architecture, and workflows. Provide clear instructions on how to set up and run the project locally. Proper documentation makes it easier for team members to onboard and contribute to the project.

12. Continuous Integration

Integrate a continuous integration (CI) system into your development workflow to automate building, testing, and deploying your Xcode projects. CI ensures that code changes do not introduce regressions and helps maintain a consistent development environment.

13. Version Control Hosting

Choose a reliable and secure hosting platform for your Git repositories. Popular options include GitHub, GitLab, and Bitbucket. Ensure that your hosting platform aligns with your project's privacy and security requirements.

14. Training and Collaboration

Invest in training and collaboration tools to help your team members become proficient in Git and Xcode's version control features. Effective communication and collaboration are key to successful version control practices.

By following these best practices, you can streamline your version control workflows in Xcode, enhance collaboration with your team, and maintain a robust and organized development process for your iOS and macOS projects.

6.5. Using External Repositories

In addition to Git repositories hosted on popular platforms like GitHub and GitLab, Xcode allows you to work with external repositories hosted elsewhere. This flexibility can be helpful in various scenarios, such as using private or self-hosted repositories or collaborating with teams using different hosting providers. In this section, we'll explore how to use external repositories in Xcode.

Cloning External Repositories

To work with an external repository in Xcode, you'll need to clone it to your local development environment. Here are the steps to clone an external repository:

1. Open Xcode and navigate to the "Source Control" menu.
2. Select "Clone" to open the cloning dialog.
3. In the dialog, provide the URL of the external repository you want to clone. This URL is typically provided by the hosting service or the repository owner.
4. Choose a destination folder on your local machine where you want to clone the repository. Xcode will create a new directory with the repository's contents in this location.
5. Optionally, you can specify the branch you want to clone or leave it empty to clone the default branch.
6. Click the "Clone" button to initiate the cloning process.

Xcode will connect to the external repository, download its contents, and create a local copy on your machine.

Managing External Repositories

Once you have cloned an external repository, you can manage it within Xcode like any other Git repository. You can create branches, make changes, commit your work, and push your changes back to the external repository when you have the necessary permissions.

Here are some common tasks when working with external repositories in Xcode:

- **Creating Branches**: Use Xcode's built-in branch management to create new branches for feature development or bug fixes within the external repository.

- **Pulling and Pushing**: Fetch changes from the external repository using the "Pull" operation and push your local changes back to it using the "Push" operation.

- **Collaboration**: Collaborate with team members who may also clone and work with the same external repository. Xcode's Git integration makes it easy to collaborate and manage changes.

- **Merging and Resolving Conflicts**: Merge branches and resolve conflicts in your local copy before pushing changes to the external repository. Xcode provides tools to help you with conflict resolution.

- **Reviewing History**: Use Xcode's version control features to review the commit history, inspect changes made by team members, and track the evolution of the external repository.

Authentication and Permissions

When working with external repositories, you may need to provide authentication credentials or SSH keys depending on the hosting service's requirements. Make sure you have the necessary permissions to push changes to the repository if it's not a public repository.

Backup and Synchronization

Since external repositories may be hosted on different platforms or services, it's essential to have a backup and synchronization strategy in place. Regularly backup your local copies of external repositories and ensure that changes made by your team are synchronized with the external repository as needed.

By using external repositories in Xcode, you can adapt your development workflow to accommodate various hosting scenarios and collaborate effectively with teams that may be using different version control platforms or services. This flexibility enhances your ability to work on a wide range of iOS and macOS projects seamlessly.

Chapter 7: Unit Testing and TDD

7.1. Introduction to Unit Testing in Xcode

Unit testing is a fundamental practice in software development that involves testing individual units or components of your code to ensure they function correctly. In Xcode, unit testing is supported through XCTest, Apple's testing framework. This section provides an introduction to unit testing in Xcode, explaining its importance, how to create and run tests, and best practices for writing effective tests.

Why Unit Testing?

Unit testing offers several advantages in the development process:

1. **Bug Detection**: Unit tests can catch bugs and issues early in the development cycle, making them easier and cheaper to fix.
2. **Regression Testing**: Tests ensure that existing functionality continues to work as expected when new code is added or changes are made.
3. **Documentation**: Tests serve as documentation for your code, making it clear how components are supposed to behave.
4. **Collaboration**: Tests enable collaboration among team members by providing a clear specification of component behavior.

Creating Unit Tests in Xcode

To create unit tests in Xcode, follow these steps:

1. Open your Xcode project.
2. In the Project Navigator, select the group or folder where you want to create your tests.
3. Go to the "File" menu, choose "New," and select "File…"
4. In the template chooser, choose "Swift File" or "Objective-C File" depending on your project's language.
5. Name the file with a suffix like "Tests" (e.g., MyComponentTests.swift).
6. In the "Targets" section, select the target for which you want to create tests, typically your app's main target.
7. Click the "Create" button.

Writing Your First Test

Once you've created a test file, you can start writing tests using XCTest. Here's an example of a simple test:

```swift
import XCTest

@testable import MyProject

class MyComponentTests: XCTestCase {

func testAddition() {

let result = add(2, 3)

XCTAssertEqual(result, 5, "Addition failed: Expected 5, but got \(result)")

}

}
```

In this example:

- We import the XCTest framework and the module we want to test (MyProject in this case).

- We define a test class that subclasses XCTestCase.

- Inside the test class, we write a test method (testAddition) that performs some action and uses assertions to check if the result is as expected.

Running Tests

To run your tests in Xcode, follow these steps:

1. Open the Test Navigator by clicking the diamond-shaped icon in the left-hand sidebar or using the shortcut Cmd+6.
2. In the Test Navigator, you'll see a list of all your test classes and methods.
3. Click the play button next to a test class or method to run the tests. Xcode will execute the tests and provide a summary of the results.

Best Practices for Writing Tests

When writing unit tests, consider the following best practices:

- **Test Isolation**: Each test should be independent and not rely on the state of other tests.

- **Test Naming**: Use descriptive test names that explain what the test is checking.

- **Arrange, Act, Assert (AAA)**: Structure your tests with a clear arrangement of data, an action, and assertions.

- **Mocking**: Use mocks and stubs to isolate the unit under test and simulate interactions with external dependencies.

- **Coverage**: Aim for high test coverage, but prioritize testing critical and complex parts of your code.

- **Continuous Integration**: Set up automated testing in your CI/CD pipeline to run tests regularly.

Unit testing is a crucial aspect of ensuring the quality and reliability of your code. By following best practices and integrating testing into your development workflow, you can build robust iOS and macOS applications with confidence.

7.2. Writing Test Cases in Swift

In the previous section, we introduced the concept of unit testing in Xcode and explained its importance. Now, let's dive deeper into writing test cases in Swift using XCTest. Writing effective test cases is essential for ensuring the reliability and correctness of your code.

Anatomy of a Test Case

A test case in XCTest is a Swift class that subclasses XCTestCase. Each test case class contains one or more test methods that check the behavior of specific code units or components. Here's the basic structure of a test case class:

```swift
import XCTest

@testable import MyProject

class MyComponentTests: XCTestCase {
    // Test methods go here
```

}

In this example:

- We import XCTest to access the testing framework.

- We use the @testable attribute to import the module we want to test (MyProject in this case).

- We define a test case class named MyComponentTests that inherits from XCTestCase.

Writing Test Methods

Test methods are the heart of your test case class. Each test method checks a specific aspect of your code's behavior. Here's an example of a simple test method:

```swift
func testAddition() {

// Arrange

let result = add(2, 3)

// Assert

XCTAssertEqual(result, 5, "Addition failed: Expected 5, but got \(result)")

}
```

In this example:

- We define a test method named testAddition.

• In the "Arrange" section, we set up the necessary data or conditions for the test. In this case, we call a hypothetical add function with two numbers.

• In the "Assert" section, we use XCTest's assertion methods to check if the result matches the expected value. Here, we use XCTAssertEqual to verify that the addition result is 5.

Assertion Methods

XCTest provides various assertion methods to check different conditions. Here are some commonly used assertion methods:

• XCTAssert(condition, message): Checks if the condition is true.

• XCTAssertTrue(condition, message): Checks if the condition is true.

• XCTAssertFalse(condition, message): Checks if the condition is false.

• XCTAssertEqual(expression1, expression2, message): Checks if two expressions are equal.

• XCTAssertNotEqual(expression1, expression2, message): Checks if two expressions are not equal.

• XCTAssertNil(expression, message): Checks if an expression is nil.

• XCTAssertNotNil(expression, message): Checks if an expression is not nil.

- XCTAssertThrowsError(expression, message): Checks if an expression throws an error.

- XCTAssertNoThrow(expression, message): Checks if an expression does not throw an error.

Testing Principles

When writing test cases, follow these principles:

1. **Test One Thing**: Each test method should focus on testing one specific aspect of your code. Avoid testing multiple behaviors in a single test method.
2. **Isolate Tests**: Ensure that tests are isolated and do not depend on the state of other tests. Use setUp and tearDown methods to set up and clean up test-specific resources.
3. **Test Edge Cases**: Test both typical and edge cases to cover a wide range of scenarios.
4. **Keep Tests Fast**: Write tests that run quickly, as developers should be able to run tests frequently during development.
5. **Regularly Refactor Tests**: As your code evolves, update and refactor your tests to keep them aligned with your code's changes.

Writing effective test cases in Swift is a key skill for iOS and macOS developers. By following best practices and thoroughly testing your code, you can improve the quality, reliability, and maintainability of your applications.

7.3. Test-Driven Development (TDD) Approach

Test-Driven Development (TDD) is a software development methodology that emphasizes writing tests before writing the actual code. In the context of iOS and macOS development with Xcode, TDD is a valuable approach to ensure code quality, maintainability, and correctness. This section explores the principles of TDD, its benefits, and how to apply it effectively in your projects.

Principles of TDD

TDD follows a simple and iterative cycle known as the Red-Green-Refactor cycle:

1. **Red**: Write a failing test case that describes the desired behavior or functionality you want to implement. At this stage, the code doesn't exist yet, so the test should fail.
2. **Green**: Write the minimum amount of code necessary to make the failing test pass. Your goal is to make the test pass as quickly as possible, not to write perfect or complete code.
3. **Refactor**: Once the test passes, refactor the code to improve its structure, readability, and maintainability while keeping all tests passing.

Repeat this cycle for each new piece of functionality or change you want to make in your application. By adhering to these principles, TDD helps ensure that your code is testable, robust, and well-designed from the beginning.

Benefits of TDD

TDD offers several advantages for iOS and macOS development:

1. **Increased Code Quality**: TDD encourages writing clean, modular, and well-structured code. Tests serve as living documentation for your code's behavior.
2. **Reduced Debugging Time**: By catching issues early in the development process, TDD reduces the time spent on debugging and fixing bugs later.
3. **Enhanced Collaboration**: Tests provide a clear specification of the expected behavior, making it easier for team members to collaborate and understand the code.
4. **Continuous Integration**: TDD fits well with continuous integration practices, allowing you to run tests automatically whenever changes are made to the codebase.
5. **Confidence in Refactoring**: With a comprehensive suite of tests, you can confidently refactor code, knowing that any regressions will be quickly identified.

Applying TDD in Xcode

To apply TDD in Xcode, follow these steps:

1. **Write a Failing Test**: Start by writing a test that describes the functionality you want to implement. Run the test, and it should fail because the functionality doesn't exist yet.
2. **Write Minimal Code**: Write the minimum code required to make the test pass. Don't worry about making the code perfect; the goal is to get a passing test.
3. **Run the Test**: After writing the code, run the test again. If it passes, you can proceed to the next step.
4. **Refactor**: Refactor the code to improve its quality. Ensure that all tests continue to pass. Refactoring can include optimizing code, improving naming, or breaking down complex methods.
5. **Repeat**: Continue this cycle for each piece of functionality

you want to implement. Gradually, your test suite will grow, providing comprehensive coverage of your code.

Here's an example of TDD in action:

Imagine you're developing a simple calculator app. You start by writing a failing test for the addition functionality. Once the test fails, you write the minimal code to make it pass. Afterward, you might write additional tests for subtraction, multiplication, and division, following the Red-Green-Refactor cycle for each operation.

```swift
func testAddition() {

let result = add(2, 3)

XCTAssertEqual(result, 5, "Addition failed: Expected 5, but got \(result)")

}
```

By adhering to TDD principles, you build a robust and reliable codebase while maintaining a high level of confidence in your application's behavior. It's a powerful approach for iOS and macOS developers that fosters code quality and agility.

7.4. Mocking and Stubbing

Mocking and stubbing are techniques used in unit testing to isolate the code being tested and control its behavior by simulating external dependencies or collaborators. These techniques are essential when you want to focus on testing a specific unit of code without invoking real external services, databases, or complex components. In this section, we'll explore the concepts of mocking and stubbing, their importance in unit testing, and how to use them effectively in Swift with XCTest.

Understanding Mock Objects

Mock objects, often referred to simply as mocks, are objects created solely for the purpose of testing. Mocks mimic the behavior of real objects but allow you to control and observe interactions with them. By using mocks, you can:

- **Isolate Dependencies**: Ensure that the code being tested doesn't rely on real external services or components.

- **Control Behavior**: Define how the mock object should behave in response to specific calls, allowing you to simulate different scenarios.

- **Verify Interactions**: Check that the code being tested interacts correctly with the mock object, such as making expected method calls.

Stubbing Methods

Stubbing is a technique used with mock objects to simulate the behavior of methods or functions without actually executing their real code. When you stub a method, you provide predefined return values or behaviors for specific inputs or conditions. This allows you to control the response of the method during testing. Here's an example in Swift:

```swift
protocol NetworkService {

func fetchData(completion: @escaping (Result<Data, Error>) -> Void)

}
```

```swift
class MockNetworkService: NetworkService {

var stubbedData: Data?

var stubbedError: Error?

func fetchData(completion: @escaping (Result<Data, Error>) ->
Void) {

if let data = stubbedData {

completion(.success(data))

} else if let error = stubbedError {

completion(.failure(error))

} else {

// Handle other cases or throw an error

}

}

}
```

In this example:

- We define a NetworkService protocol with a fetchData
method that takes a completion handler.

- We create a MockNetworkService class that conforms
to the protocol and implements the fetchData method.

- The MockNetworkService allows us to stub the data
and error values, controlling the behavior of the method
during testing.

Benefits of Mocking and Stubbing

Mocking and stubbing provide several benefits in unit testing:

1. **Isolation**: By replacing real external dependencies with mock objects, you isolate the code being tested, ensuring that it operates independently of external services or components.
2. **Control**: You have full control over the behavior of mock objects, enabling you to simulate different scenarios, edge cases, and error conditions.
3. **Predictable Testing**: Stubbing allows you to predict the responses of methods or functions, making your tests more predictable and reliable.
4. **Speed**: Testing with mock objects is often faster than interacting with real external services or databases, improving test execution speed.
5. **Reduced Flakiness**: Mocking eliminates external factors that can introduce flakiness in tests, such as network connectivity or server availability.

In conclusion, mocking and stubbing are valuable techniques for unit testing in Swift. They help you write focused, isolated tests that verify the behavior of your code while minimizing dependencies on external services or components. By using mocks and stubs effectively, you can ensure the reliability and maintainability of your codebase.

7.5. Continuous Integration and Testing

Continuous Integration (CI) and Continuous Testing are integral parts of modern software development practices. They aim to ensure that your code is consistently tested, integrated, and validated throughout the development process. In this section, we'll explore the concepts of CI and continuous testing in the context of iOS development using Xcode.

Understanding Continuous Integration (CI)

Continuous Integration is a software development practice where code changes are automatically built, tested, and integrated into the project's main codebase whenever changes are pushed to a version control repository, such as Git. The key principles of CI include:

- **Automated Builds**: The code is compiled and built automatically whenever there are new changes.

- **Automated Testing**: A suite of automated tests, including unit tests and integration tests, is executed to verify that the code changes didn't introduce regressions.

- **Frequent Integration**: Changes are regularly integrated into the main codebase, reducing the risk of integration conflicts and ensuring a consistently functioning application.

Setting Up CI in Xcode

Xcode provides built-in support for configuring CI workflows using tools like Xcode Server, Jenkins, Travis CI, or GitHub Actions. The typical CI process for an iOS project involves the following steps:

1. **Code Changes**: Developers push code changes to a version control repository, triggering the CI process.
2. **Build and Test**: The CI server automatically fetches the latest code, builds the application, and runs a suite of automated tests, including unit tests, UI tests, and any

other custom tests.

3. **Reporting**: The CI server generates reports and notifications, indicating whether the build and tests were successful or if any issues were detected.
4. **Deployment**: Depending on the project's configuration, successful builds can be deployed to testing or production environments.

Benefits of Continuous Integration

Continuous Integration offers several benefits to iOS development:

1. **Early Issue Detection**: CI helps detect issues and bugs early in the development process, reducing the cost of fixing them.
2. **Consistency**: It ensures that the codebase is always in a buildable and testable state, promoting code consistency and reliability.
3. **Automated Testing**: Automated testing ensures that the application functions as expected after each code change, reducing the risk of regressions.
4. **Efficient Collaboration**: CI encourages frequent code integration, facilitating efficient collaboration among team members.
5. **Deployment Confidence**: Successful CI builds instill confidence in the deployment process, as tested builds are ready for release.

Continuous Testing in Xcode

Continuous Testing in Xcode involves running your unit tests and UI tests automatically during the CI process. Xcode's testing features, such as XCTest and XCUITest, are tightly integrated with CI workflows. Here are some key points to consider:

- XCTest: XCTest is Apple's built-in testing framework for writing unit tests in Swift or Objective-C. You can configure your CI server to execute XCTest test suites as part of the CI process.

- XCUITest: XCUITest is used for UI testing in Xcode. It allows you to automate interactions with your app's user interface. You can integrate XCUITest tests into your CI pipeline to verify the functionality of your app's UI.

- Code Coverage: Xcode provides code coverage metrics, showing which portions of your code are exercised by your tests. Monitoring code coverage in CI helps ensure comprehensive testing.

Conclusion

Continuous Integration and Continuous Testing are essential practices in iOS development, ensuring that your code is consistently tested and integrated throughout the development lifecycle. By setting up CI workflows and automating testing, you can catch issues early, maintain code quality, and improve collaboration within your development team. Xcode provides the necessary tools and integration options to streamline the CI and testing process for iOS projects.

Chapter 8: Advanced Interface Building

8.1. Animations and Transitions

In iOS app development, creating smooth and engaging animations and transitions can greatly enhance the user experience. Animations make your app more interactive and visually appealing, providing feedback and guiding the user's attention. This section will explore the concepts of animations and transitions in iOS using Swift and Xcode.

Understanding Animations

Animations involve changing the properties of UI elements over time to create the illusion of motion or transformation. In iOS, you can animate various properties like position, size, opacity, and color. The UIView class provides powerful animation capabilities through the UIView.animate(withDuration:animations:) method.

Here's a basic example of animating a view's position:

```
UIView.animate(withDuration: 0.5) {

myView.frame.origin.x += 100

}
```

In this code snippet, myView moves 100 points to the right over a duration of 0.5 seconds. You can also specify additional options like easing curves and completion handlers to customize animations further.

Transitions Between View Controllers

Transitions come into play when you navigate between different view controllers in your app. iOS provides built-in transition styles like push, modal, and custom transitions. These transitions define how one view controller transitions to another.

For instance, to push a view controller onto a navigation stack:

let viewController = MyViewController()

navigationController?.pushViewController(viewController, animated: **true**)

In this case, the animated parameter controls whether the transition is animated or not. You can also customize the transition animations by implementing custom transitions and using the UIViewControllerTransitioningDelegate protocol.

Auto Layout and Animations

When working with animations, it's essential to consider Auto Layout, which dynamically adjusts your UI elements based on different screen sizes and orientations. To animate constraints, you can create @IBOutlets for your constraints and modify their constant values within an animation block.

myConstraint.constant = 100 // *Change the constraint's constant value*

UIView.animate(withDuration: 0.5) {

self.view.layoutIfNeeded() // *Update the layout*

}

By updating constraints inside an animation block and calling layoutIfNeeded(), you ensure that the changes are smoothly animated.

Advanced Animation Techniques

iOS offers various advanced animation techniques, such as keyframe animations, interactive animations, and physics-based animations. Keyframe animations allow you to create complex animations by specifying multiple keyframes with different properties and timings.

Interactive animations enable users to control animations using gestures like swipe or pinch. Physics-based animations simulate real-world physics, making animations feel natural and responsive.

Conclusion

Animations and transitions are vital tools in iOS app development, providing a dynamic and engaging user experience. Whether you're animating UI elements or creating seamless transitions between view controllers, understanding animation principles and utilizing the animation APIs in Swift and Xcode will help you build visually appealing and user-friendly iOS applications.

8.2. Custom View Controllers

In iOS app development, view controllers are at the core of creating the user interface and managing the flow of your application. While Apple provides a variety of built-in view controllers like UITableViewController and UICollectionViewController, there are situations where you'll need to create custom view controllers tailored to your app's specific needs. This section will delve into the creation and customization of custom view controllers in Swift and Xcode.

Creating a Custom View Controller

To create a custom view controller, you typically subclass UIViewController and then design its associated user interface using Interface Builder or programmatically. Here's a basic outline of how to create a custom view controller:

import UIKit

class CustomViewController: UIViewController {

override func viewDidLoad() {

super.viewDidLoad()

// Additional setup code

}

// Implement other view lifecycle methods and functionality here

}

In this example, CustomViewController is a subclass of UIViewController. You can override various methods like viewDidLoad() to perform setup tasks when the view controller is loaded.

Designing the User Interface

You have two main options for designing the user interface of your custom view controller:

1. **Using Interface Builder:** You can use Xcode's Interface Builder to design the interface visually. Create a corresponding XIB (Interface Builder) file for your view controller, connect outlets, and design your user interface

elements.

2. **Programmatic UI:** If you prefer to create the interface entirely in code, you can do so by overriding the loadView() method and setting up your views programmatically. This gives you full control over the UI.

Segues and Storyboards

If your app uses storyboards for navigation, you can create segues between view controllers to define the flow of your app. Segues allow you to transition from one view controller to another, passing data between them if needed. You can create custom segues for more advanced transitions.

Navigation Controller and Tab Bar Controller

Often, custom view controllers are used within navigation controllers or tab bar controllers to manage navigation and tab-based interfaces. You can embed your custom view controller in a navigation controller or connect it to a tab bar controller within Interface Builder.

Communication Between View Controllers

In iOS development, it's common for view controllers to communicate with each other. You can achieve this by defining protocols, using delegates, or passing data between view controllers directly.

Custom Transition Animations

To create custom transition animations when presenting or dismissing view controllers, you can adopt the UIViewControllerTransitioningDelegate protocol. This allows you to specify the animations and interactions for transitioning between view controllers.

Conclusion

Custom view controllers are essential for building iOS applications that meet your specific requirements. Whether you're designing the user interface visually with Interface Builder or programmatically, creating custom transitions, or facilitating communication between view controllers, mastering the art of custom view controllers will empower you to build feature-rich and user-friendly iOS apps.

8.3. Gestures and Interactions

In modern iOS app development, user interactions play a crucial role in creating engaging and intuitive applications. Gestures and interactions enable users to interact with the app through touches, swipes, pinches, and other input methods. This section explores how to implement gestures and interactions in your iOS app using Swift and Xcode.

Gesture Recognizers

Gesture recognizers are essential components for detecting and responding to user interactions. iOS provides a variety of gesture recognizers, including:

- **UITapGestureRecognizer**: Recognizes single or multiple taps on a view.

- **UIPinchGestureRecognizer**: Detects pinching gestures for zooming.

- **UIPanGestureRecognizer**: Tracks dragging and panning gestures.

- **UISwipeGestureRecognizer**: Recognizes swipes in different directions.

- **UIRotationGestureRecognizer**: Detects rotation gestures.

- **UILongPressGestureRecognizer**: Identifies long-press gestures.

- **UIEdgePanGestureRecognizer**: Recognizes edge pan gestures.

You can add gesture recognizers to your views and define actions to perform when a gesture is recognized.

```swift
let tapGesture = UITapGestureRecognizer(target: self, action: #selector(handleTap))

myView.addGestureRecognizer(tapGesture)

@objc func handleTap() {

// Handle the tap gesture here

}
```

Gesture Delegation

Sometimes, you may need more control over gesture recognition, such as recognizing multiple gestures simultaneously or handling complex interactions. In such cases, you can implement gesture delegation by conforming to the UIGestureRecognizerDelegate protocol.

```swift
class MyViewController: UIViewController, UIGestureRecognizerDelegate {

override func viewDidLoad() {

super.viewDidLoad()

let panGesture = UIPanGestureRecognizer(target: self, action: #selector(handlePan))

panGesture.delegate = self

myView.addGestureRecognizer(panGesture)

}

@objc func handlePan(_ gesture: UIPanGestureRecognizer) {

// Handle the pan gesture

}

func gestureRecognizer(_ gestureRecognizer: UIGestureRecognizer, shouldRecognizeSimultaneouslyWith otherGestureRecognizer: UIGestureRecognizer) -> Bool {

// Allow multiple gestures to be recognized simultaneously

return true

}

}
```

Interactive Animations

Gestures can be used to drive interactive animations, allowing users to control elements on the screen. For example, you can use pan gestures to move objects, pinch gestures to zoom in and out, or swipe gestures to navigate through a photo gallery.

To create interactive animations, update the view's properties within the gesture handler based on the user's input. You can use the gesture's state to determine when the interaction begins, continues, or ends.

Complex Interactions

Complex interactions may involve combining multiple gestures, such as pinch-to-zoom and pan-to-move simultaneously. By carefully managing the recognition and coordination of these gestures, you can create rich and responsive user experiences.

Conclusion

Gestures and interactions are fundamental components of user interface design in iOS. Whether you're implementing simple tap gestures or complex multi-touch interactions, understanding how to use gesture recognizers and delegate methods will allow you to create responsive and user-friendly iOS applications.

8.4. Working with Table Views and Collection Views

Table views and collection views are fundamental components for displaying structured data in iOS applications. They allow you to present information in a scrollable, organized manner, making them essential for various app interfaces. This section explores working with table views and collection views in Swift and Xcode.

Table Views

Creating a Table View

To create a table view, you'll typically use UITableView in your view controller. You can add a table view either programmatically or through Interface Builder. Here's how to create one programmatically:

import UIKit

class MyTableViewController: UITableViewController {

override func viewDidLoad() {

super.viewDidLoad()

// Set the data source and delegate

tableView.dataSource = **self**

tableView.delegate = **self**

}

}

Populating Data

To populate data in a table view, you need to implement the UITableViewDataSource protocol methods. These methods specify the number of sections, rows in each section, and provide cell content.

extension MyTableViewController {

```swift
override func numberOfSections(in tableView: UITableView) -> Int {

return 1

}

override func tableView(_ tableView: UITableView, numberOfRowsInSection section: Int) -> Int {

return data.count // Replace 'data' with your data source

}

override func tableView(_ tableView: UITableView, cellForRowAt indexPath: IndexPath) -> UITableViewCell {

let cell = tableView.dequeueReusableCell(withIdentifier: "Cell", for: indexPath)

cell.textLabel?.text = data[indexPath.row] // Replace 'data' with your data source

return cell

}

}
```

Handling Selection

You can respond to user selections by implementing the UITableViewDelegate method tableView(_:didSelectRowAt:). This method is called when a cell is tapped.

```swift
extension MyTableViewController {
```

```swift
override func tableView(_ tableView: UITableView,
didSelectRowAt indexPath: IndexPath) {

let selectedData = data[indexPath.row] // Replace 'data' with your data source

// Handle the selection

}

}
```

Collection Views

Creating a Collection View

Collection views are created similarly to table views. You can add a collection view either programmatically or through Interface Builder. Here's a basic programmatic setup:

```swift
import UIKit

class MyCollectionViewController: UICollectionViewController {

override func viewDidLoad() {

super.viewDidLoad()

// Set the data source and delegate

collectionView.dataSource = self

collectionView.delegate = self

}

}
```

Populating Data

Populating data in a collection view is similar to a table view. You implement the UICollectionViewDataSource protocol methods to specify the number of sections, items in each section, and provide cell content.

```swift
extension MyCollectionViewController {

override func numberOfSections(in collectionView: UICollectionView) -> Int {

return 1

}

override func collectionView(_ collectionView: UICollectionView, numberOfItemsInSection section: Int) -> Int {

return data.count // Replace 'data' with your data source

}

override func collectionView(_ collectionView: UICollectionView, cellForItemAt indexPath: IndexPath) -> UICollectionViewCell {

let cell = collectionView.dequeueReusableCell(withReuseIdentifier: "Cell", for: indexPath) as! MyCollectionViewCell

cell.textLabel.text = data[indexPath.item] // Replace 'data' with your data source

return cell

}

}
```

Handling Selection

Handling selection in a collection view is done by implementing the UICollectionViewDelegate method collectionView(_:didSelectItemAt:).

extension MyCollectionViewController {

override func collectionView(_ collectionView: UICollectionView, didSelectItemAt indexPath: IndexPath) {

let selectedData = data[indexPath.item] *// Replace 'data' with your data source*

// Handle the selection

}

}

Conclusion

Table views and collection views are powerful tools for presenting data in iOS applications. Whether you choose a table view for a list-based interface or a collection view for more flexible layouts, understanding their usage and implementing the required data source and delegate methods will allow you to create dynamic and interactive user interfaces.

8.5. Accessibility and Internationalization

Accessibility and internationalization are critical aspects of iOS app development to ensure a wide user base and compliance with global standards. In this section, we'll explore how to make your app accessible to users with disabilities and how to prepare it for multiple languages and regions.

Accessibility

Enabling VoiceOver

VoiceOver is a screen-reading feature on iOS devices that allows visually impaired users to interact with apps. To ensure your app works well with VoiceOver, follow these guidelines:

1. **Use Descriptive Labels**: Assign meaningful labels and hints to UI elements using the accessibilityLabel and accessibilityHint properties.
2. **Accessible Fonts**: Use system fonts with dynamic type support to ensure text is resizable for users with different visual needs.
3. **Focus Order**: Ensure that the focus order (tab order) of elements in your UI makes sense when navigating with VoiceOver.
4. **Traits**: Set appropriate accessibility traits (e.g., button, link, header) for UI elements to provide context to VoiceOver.
5. **Testing**: Regularly test your app with VoiceOver enabled to identify and fix accessibility issues.

Dynamic Type

iOS offers dynamic type support, allowing users to adjust the text size to their preferences. Ensure your app's text is resizable by using system fonts and respecting content size categories.

```
label.font = UIFont.preferredFont(forTextStyle: .body)
```

Internationalization (i18n) and Localization (l10n)

Preparing for Multiple Languages

To make your app accessible to a global audience, internationalization is crucial. Follow these steps:

1. **Extract Localizable Text**: Use NSLocalizedString to wrap any text that needs to be translated.

```
let localizedString = NSLocalizedString("key", comment: "Description")
```

1. **Create Localization Files**: Generate .strings files for each supported language using the genstrings command or Xcode's built-in tools.
2. **Translate**: Replace the English text in each .strings file with the corresponding translation.
3. **Select Language**: iOS will automatically load the appropriate localization based on the user's device language settings.

Handling RTL Languages

For right-to-left (RTL) languages like Arabic and Hebrew, ensure that your app's UI adapts correctly. Use auto layout and constraint priorities to control the layout direction.

```
if UIApplication.shared.userInterfaceLayoutDirection == .rightToLeft {

// Adjust layout for RTL

}
```

Localization Testing

Test your app thoroughly in different languages and regions to ensure text doesn't get cut off, buttons remain functional, and the overall user experience remains consistent.

Conclusion

Accessibility and internationalization are essential considerations for iOS app development. By making your app accessible to all users, regardless of disabilities, and providing support for multiple languages and regions, you can reach a broader audience and deliver a better user experience. Properly implementing these features will help your app comply with global accessibility standards and expand its reach to users worldwide.

9.1. Understanding Data Persistence

Data persistence is a fundamental aspect of app development, allowing your iOS applications to store and manage data effectively. Whether it's user preferences, app settings, or user-generated content, knowing how to handle data persistence is crucial. In this section, we'll explore various data persistence techniques available in iOS.

UserDefaults

UserDefaults is a simple way to store small amounts of data, such as user preferences and settings. It provides a key-value storage mechanism and is easy to use.

```
// Saving a value
```

```
UserDefaults.standard.set("John", forKey: "userName")
```

```
// Retrieving a value

if let userName = UserDefaults.standard.string(forKey: "userName") {

print("User's name: \(userName)")

}
```

File System

You can store data in files within your app's sandboxed file system. This is suitable for more substantial data, such as documents or user-generated content.

```
// Getting the document directory URL

if let documentDirectory = FileManager.default.urls(for: .documentDirectory, in: .userDomainMask).first {

let fileURL = documentDirectory.appendingPathComponent("data.txt")

// Writing to a file

do {

try "Hello, World!".write(to: fileURL, atomically: true, encoding: .utf8)

} catch {

print("Error writing to file: \(error)")

}

// Reading from a file
```

```swift
if let contents = try? String(contentsOf: fileURL) {

print("File contents: \(contents)")

}

}
```

CoreData

CoreData is a powerful framework for managing object graphs and persisting data in a structured way. It's suitable for handling complex data models and relationships.

import CoreData

```swift
// Initializing CoreData stack

let container = NSPersistentContainer(name: "DataModel")

container.loadPersistentStores { (_, error) in

if let error = error {

fatalError("CoreData initialization failed: \(error)")

}

}

// Creating a managed object

let context = container.viewContext

if let entity = NSEntityDescription.entity(forEntityName: "Person",
in: context),

let person = NSManagedObject(entity: entity, insertInto: context)
as? Person {
```

```swift
person.name = "Alice"

person.age = 30

// Saving the context

do {

try context.save()

} catch {

print("Error saving context: \(error)")

}

}
```

Keychain

The Keychain is a secure way to store sensitive information like passwords, tokens, or encryption keys. It's suitable for protecting confidential data.

```swift
import Security

// Saving a password to Keychain

let password = "secretpassword".data(using: .utf8)!

let query: [String: Any] = [

kSecClass as String: kSecClassGenericPassword,

kSecAttrAccount as String: "myAccount",

kSecValueData as String: password

]
```

```swift
let status = SecItemAdd(query as CFDictionary, nil)

if status == errSecSuccess {

print("Password saved successfully")

}

// Retrieving a password from Keychain

var query = query

query[kSecReturnData as String] = true

var result: AnyObject?

let status = SecItemCopyMatching(query as CFDictionary, &result)

if status == errSecSuccess, let passwordData = result as? Data, let password = String(data: passwordData, encoding: .utf8) {

print("Retrieved password: \(password)")

}
```

UserDefaults vs. File System vs. CoreData vs. Keychain

Choosing the right data persistence method depends on your app's requirements. UserDefaults is suitable for simple settings, while the file system is more versatile for various data types. CoreData provides a structured approach for complex data models, and the Keychain offers security for sensitive information. Understanding these options will help you make informed decisions when implementing data persistence in your iOS app.

9.2. Core Data Fundamentals

Core Data is a powerful framework provided by Apple for managing and persisting data in iOS and macOS applications. It offers a high-level, object-oriented API for interacting with data and is especially useful for managing complex data models with relationships. In this section, we will explore the fundamentals of Core Data.

Core Data Stack

The Core Data stack consists of the following components:

1. **Managed Object Model (MOM):** It defines the data model and entity relationships in your application. You can design your data model using Xcode's visual editor.
2. **Persistent Store Coordinator (PSC):** This component manages the interaction between your app and the underlying persistent store. It handles reading and writing data to the storage.
3. **Managed Object Context (MOC):** MOC is responsible for managing a set of managed objects, which represent the data in your app. It acts as a scratchpad for changes before they are saved to the persistent store.
4. **Persistent Store:** This is where the data is actually stored. It can be an SQLite database, XML, or binary format, depending on your configuration.

Creating a Core Data Model

To get started with Core Data, you first need to create a data model. You can do this by adding a Core Data Data Model file (.xcdatamodeld) to your Xcode project. In this model, you define entities, attributes, and relationships between them.

Creating Entities and Attributes

Entities represent objects in your data model. For example, if you are building a task management app, you might have an "Task" entity with attributes like "title," "dueDate," and "isCompleted."

```
import CoreData

class Task: NSManagedObject {

@NSManaged var title: String?

@NSManaged var dueDate: Date?

@NSManaged var isCompleted: Bool

}
```

Fetching Data with NSFetchRequest

To retrieve data from Core Data, you use NSFetchRequest. It allows you to define criteria for fetching objects, such as filtering, sorting, and limiting the results.

```
let fetchRequest: NSFetchRequest<Task> = Task.fetchRequest()

fetchRequest.predicate = NSPredicate(format: "isCompleted == %@", NSNumber(value: false))

fetchRequest.sortDescriptors = [NSSortDescriptor(key: "dueDate", ascending: true)]

do {

let incompleteTasks = try managedObjectContext.fetch(fetchRequest)

for task in incompleteTasks {
```

```swift
print("Task: \(task.title ?? "No Title")")

}

} catch {

print("Error fetching data: \(error)")

}
```

Adding and Deleting Objects

You can create new managed objects and add them to the context for insertion into the persistent store. Similarly, you can delete objects by removing them from the context and saving the changes.

```swift
let newTask = Task(context: managedObjectContext)

newTask.title = "Finish Core Data section"

newTask.dueDate = Date()

newTask.isCompleted = false

do {

try managedObjectContext.save()

} catch {

print("Error saving new task: \(error)")

}

managedObjectContext.delete(taskToDelete)

do {

try managedObjectContext.save()
```

```
} catch {

print("Error deleting task: \(error)")

}
```

Updating and Saving Data

Once you make changes to managed objects, you can save those changes to the persistent store using the managed object context's save() method.

```
task.isCompleted = true

do {

try managedObjectContext.save()

} catch {

print("Error saving updated task: \(error)")

}
```

Core Data Relationships

Core Data allows you to define relationships between entities. For example, you can create a "Project" entity and establish a to-many relationship with "Task" entities to represent a project with multiple tasks.

```
import CoreData

class Project: NSManagedObject {

@NSManaged var title: String?

@NSManaged var tasks: Set<Task>
```

```
}
```

```
let project = Project(context: managedObjectContext)
```

```
project.title = "iOS App Development"
```

```
project.addToTasks(task1)
```

```
project.addToTasks(task2)
```

In this example, a project can have multiple tasks associated with it.

Conclusion

Core Data is a robust and flexible framework for data persistence in iOS and macOS applications. Understanding its core components, creating data models, and performing basic CRUD operations are essential skills for any iOS developer.

9.3. Managing Databases with SQLite

SQLite is a popular and lightweight relational database management system (RDBMS) that is often used as the default persistent store for Core Data in iOS and macOS applications. In this section, we will explore how Core Data interacts with SQLite and how to manage databases effectively.

SQLite as the Persistent Store

When you choose Core Data as your data persistence framework, you can configure it to use different types of persistent stores. SQLite is a common choice because it provides a structured and efficient way to store data locally on the device.

Core Data abstracts the interaction with SQLite, allowing you to work with managed objects and entities without writing SQL queries directly. Under the hood, Core Data handles SQL generation and execution for you.

Database File Location

The SQLite database file used by Core Data is typically located in the app's sandboxed file system. The exact file path depends on your app's configuration and is usually found in the Application Support directory.

You can programmatically obtain the URL of the SQLite database file using the following code:

```
let storeURL = FileManager.default.urls(for: .applicationSupportDirectory, in: .userDomainMask).first!.appendingPathComponent("YourApp.sqlite")
```

Database Schema

SQLite stores data in tables, and the structure of these tables is determined by your Core Data data model. Each entity in your data model corresponds to a table in the SQLite database, and each attribute maps to a column.

Core Data automatically creates and manages the database schema based on your data model. When you make changes to your data model (e.g., adding, deleting, or modifying entities and attributes), Core Data can perform automatic lightweight migrations to update the schema without data loss.

Lightweight vs. Heavyweight Migrations

Core Data provides two types of migrations: lightweight and heavyweight.

- **Lightweight Migration:** This type of migration is performed automatically by Core Data when the changes to the data model are compatible. For example, adding a new attribute or entity is typically a lightweight migration.

- **Heavyweight Migration:** If your data model changes are more complex, such as renaming an entity or changing a relationship, you may need to perform a heavyweight migration manually. This involves creating a mapping model to guide the migration process.

Database Operations

Core Data makes it easy to perform database operations such as inserting, updating, and deleting records. These operations are typically done through the managed object context.

```swift
let newTask = Task(context: managedObjectContext)

newTask.title = "New Task"

newTask.dueDate = Date()

newTask.isCompleted = false

do {

try managedObjectContext.save()

} catch {

print("Error saving new task: \(error)")

}
```

Conclusion

SQLite is a reliable and efficient choice for the persistent store in Core Data applications. Understanding how Core Data interacts with SQLite, where the database file is located, and how to handle schema changes and migrations is crucial for building robust and data-driven iOS and macOS apps.

9.4. Networking and API Integration

In modern iOS and macOS applications, networking and API integration play a crucial role in connecting your app to remote servers and services. This section explores the fundamentals of networking, making HTTP requests, and integrating APIs into your Swift-based applications.

Networking Basics

Networking in iOS and macOS revolves around the URLSession class, which provides a flexible and powerful API for making network requests. Here's a basic example of how to create and use a URLSession to make a simple GET request:

```swift
let url = URL(string: "https://api.example.com/data")!

let task = URLSession.shared.dataTask(with: url) { (data, response, error) in

if let error = error {

print("Error: \(error)")

return

}
```

```swift
if let data = data {

// Process the data here

}

}

task.resume()
```

Making API Requests

When working with APIs, you'll often need to include additional information in your requests, such as headers, query parameters, or request bodies. Here's an example of making a POST request with JSON data:

```swift
let url = URL(string: "https://api.example.com/post")!

var request = URLRequest(url: url)

request.httpMethod = "POST"

request.setValue("application/json", forHTTPHeaderField: "Content-Type")

let jsonData = try? JSONSerialization.data(withJSONObject: ["key": "value"])

request.httpBody = jsonData

let task = URLSession.shared.dataTask(with: request) { (data, response, error) in

if let error = error {

print("Error: \(error)")
```

```
return

}

if let data = data {

// Process the response data here

}

}

task.resume()
```

Handling API Responses

When you receive a response from an API, you'll typically parse the data into meaningful Swift objects. Popular libraries like JSONDecoder can help you decode JSON responses into Swift structs or classes easily.

```
struct Post: Codable {

let userId: Int

let id: Int

let title: String

let body: String

}

let url = URL(string: "https://jsonplaceholder.typicode.com/posts/1")!

let task = URLSession.shared.dataTask(with: url) { (data, response, error) in
```

```swift
if let error = error {

print("Error: \(error)")

return

}

if let data = data {

do {

let post = try JSONDecoder().decode(Post.self, from: data)

print("Post title: \(post.title)")

} catch {

print("Error decoding JSON: \(error)")

}

}

}

task.resume()
```

Error Handling and Best Practices

When working with networking and APIs, error handling is crucial. Always handle errors gracefully and consider implementing retry mechanisms or caching for a more robust app.

Additionally, consider security best practices such as using HTTPS for secure communication and securely storing sensitive information such as API keys.

Conclusion

Networking and API integration are essential skills for iOS and macOS developers. By understanding the basics of making network requests, handling responses, and following best practices, you can create applications that interact seamlessly with remote services and provide valuable data to your users.

9.5. Working with JSON and XML

In modern app development, working with data often involves exchanging information in JSON (JavaScript Object Notation) or XML (eXtensible Markup Language) formats. These formats are commonly used for data serialization and communication with external services. In this section, we will explore how to work with JSON and XML data in your iOS and macOS applications using Swift.

Parsing JSON Data

JSON is a lightweight data-interchange format that is easy to read and write for both humans and machines. Swift provides built-in support for working with JSON data through the JSONSerialization class.

Parsing JSON from a String

```swift
let jsonString = """
{
"name": "John Doe",
"age": 30,
```

```swift
  "city": "New York"

}
"""

if let data = jsonString.data(using: .utf8) {

do {

if let json = try JSONSerialization.jsonObject(with: data, options:
[]) as? [String: Any] {

let name = json["name"] as? String

let age = json["age"] as? Int

let city = json["city"] as? String

print("Name: \(name ?? "N/A"), Age: \(age ?? -1), City: \(city ?? "N/
A")")

}

} catch {

print("Error parsing JSON: \(error)")

}

}
```

Parsing JSON from a File

```swift
if let path = Bundle.main.path(forResource: "data", ofType: "json") {

do {
```

```swift
let data = try Data(contentsOf: URL(fileURLWithPath: path))

if let json = try JSONSerialization.jsonObject(with: data, options:
[]) as? [String: Any] {

// Process JSON data here

}

} catch {

print("Error reading JSON file: \(error)")

}

}
```

Parsing XML Data

XML is a markup language used for structuring and storing data. While Swift doesn't provide built-in XML parsing, you can use third-party libraries like SWXMLHash or XMLParser to work with XML data.

Parsing XML with SWXMLHash

```swift
import SWXMLHash

let xmlString = """

<person>

<name>John Doe</name>

<age>30</age>

<city>New York</city>
```

```
</person>
"""

if let xmlData = xmlString.data(using: .utf8) {
    let xml = SWXMLHash.parse(xmlData)
    let name = xml["person"]["name"].element?.text
    let age = Int(xml["person"]["age"].element?.text ?? "0")
    let city = xml["person"]["city"].element?.text
    print("Name: \(name ?? "N/A"), Age: \(age ?? -1), City: \(city ?? "N/A")")
}
```

Parsing XML with XMLParser

```
import Foundation

class MyXMLParserDelegate: NSObject, XMLParserDelegate {
    var currentElement: String?
    var name: String?
    var age: String?
    var city: String?

    func parser(_ parser: XMLParser, didStartElement elementName:
    String, namespaceURI: String?, qualifiedName qName: String?,
    attributes attributeDict: [String : String] = [:]) {
        currentElement = elementName
```

```swift
}

func parser(_ parser: XMLParser, foundCharacters string: String) {

switch currentElement {

case "name":

name = string

case "age":

age = string

case "city":

city = string

default:

break

}

}

func parser(_ parser: XMLParser, didEndElement elementName: String, namespaceURI: String?, qualifiedName qName: String?) {

if elementName == "person" {

print("Name: \(name ?? "N/A"), Age: \(age ?? "N/A"), City: \(city ?? "N/A")")

}

}

}
```

```swift
let xmlString = """
<person>
<name>John Doe</name>
<age>30</age>
<city>New York</city>
</person>
"""

if let data = xmlString.data(using: .utf8) {
let parser = XMLParser(data: data)
let delegate = MyXMLParserDelegate()
parser.delegate = delegate
parser.parse()
}
```

Conclusion

Working with JSON and XML data is a common task in iOS and macOS development when interacting with web services or handling structured data. Swift provides built-in support for JSON, while third-party libraries can help you parse XML data efficiently. Understanding these data formats and their parsing methods is essential for building robust and data-driven applications.

Chapter 10: Distributing Your App

10.1. Preparing Your App for Distribution

Distributing your iOS or macOS app to users is an exciting milestone in your development journey. Whether you're targeting the App Store, enterprise deployment, or ad-hoc distribution, proper preparation is crucial to ensure a seamless user experience. In this section, we'll explore the steps involved in preparing your app for distribution.

Code Signing and Provisioning Profiles

Before you can distribute your app, it must be signed with a valid code signing certificate and associated with the appropriate provisioning profile. Code signing ensures that your app is authentic and hasn't been tampered with. Provisioning profiles specify which devices or users can run your app.

1. Apple Developer Account

Ensure that you have a valid Apple Developer account. You'll need this to create and manage provisioning profiles and certificates. If you don't have one, you can enroll in the Apple Developer Program on the Apple Developer website[1].

2. Xcode Setup

In Xcode, go to **Preferences > Accounts** and make sure your Apple Developer account is added. Xcode will automatically manage your provisioning profiles and certificates.

---

1. https://developer.apple.com/

3. Create an App ID

An App ID is a unique identifier for your app. You can create one on the Apple Developer website under **Identifiers > App IDs**. Make sure to choose the appropriate options, such as enabling app services like push notifications or in-app purchases, based on your app's requirements.

4. Generate a Certificate

To sign your app, you'll need a code signing certificate. In Xcode, under **Preferences > Accounts**, select your team and click the "Manage Certificates" button. Create or download the necessary certificates.

5. Create a Provisioning Profile

Provisioning profiles define how your app can be distributed. You can create them on the Apple Developer website under **Profiles > All**. Choose the type of provisioning profile that matches your distribution method: App Store, Ad Hoc, or Development.

6. Configure Xcode Project

In your Xcode project settings, select the provisioning profile you created in the **Signing & Capabilities** tab. Xcode will handle the code signing process during the build.

App Store Connect

If you're planning to distribute your app on the App Store, you'll need to set up an App Store Connect account and create a listing for your app. Here are the steps:

1. App Store Connect Account

Log in to App Store Connect[2] with your Apple ID associated with your developer account. You may need to agree to the latest terms and conditions.

2. Create an App Listing

Click on **My Apps** and then the "+" button to create a new app listing. Follow the on-screen instructions to provide all the required information, including the app's name, description, icon, and screenshots.

3. App Store Review Guidelines

Familiarize yourself with the App Store Review Guidelines to ensure your app complies with Apple's policies and requirements. Non-compliance can result in rejection or removal from the App Store.

4. App Pricing and Availability

Set the pricing and availability of your app based on your business model and target markets. You can also configure app availability for pre-orders.

5. App Builds and Versions

In App Store Connect, you can manage multiple app versions, including pre-release builds for testing and development. Ensure that your app meets all requirements before submitting it for review.

---

2. https://appstoreconnect.apple.com/

Testing and Quality Assurance

Before distributing your app, thorough testing and quality assurance (QA) are essential to identify and fix any issues. Here are some testing aspects to consider:

1. Device Compatibility

Test your app on various iOS and macOS devices and versions to ensure compatibility. Use the Xcode simulator and physical devices for testing.

2. Performance Testing

Check your app's performance, responsiveness, and memory usage. Use profiling tools like Instruments to identify and address bottlenecks.

3. User Experience

Verify that your app's user interface is intuitive, adheres to design guidelines, and provides a smooth user experience.

4. Functional Testing

Test all app features, including navigation, input validation, data retrieval, and data submission. Verify that all functionality works as expected.

5. Security Testing

Identify and fix security vulnerabilities in your app, such as data encryption, authentication, and network security.

6. Beta Testing

Consider conducting beta testing with a group of trusted users or using Apple's TestFlight service to gather feedback and identify issues.

App Submission and Review

Once your app is thoroughly tested and ready for distribution, you can submit it to the App Store or deploy it using other distribution methods. Here's an overview of the submission process:

1. Prepare App Assets

Ensure you have all required assets, including app icons, screenshots, and promotional materials, ready for submission.

2. Submit App for Review

In App Store Connect, select the app version you want to submit and click the "Submit for Review" button. Fill in all required information and respond to any prompts.

3. App Review Process

Apple will review your app to ensure it complies with guidelines and policies. The review process may take several days, depending on the volume of submissions.

4. App Approval

If your app passes the review, it will be approved for the App Store. You'll receive a notification, and your app will be available to users based on the release date you specified.

5. Distribution

Once approved, your app will be accessible to users through the App Store. You can also manage app updates and monitor its performance using App Store Connect.

Alternative Distribution Methods

Apart from the App Store, you may want to distribute your app through other methods, such as enterprise distribution, ad-hoc distribution, or external repositories. Each method has its own requirements and limitations, so be sure to research and follow the appropriate procedures.

Conclusion

Preparing your app for distribution is a crucial step in bringing your creation to a wider audience. Whether you're targeting the App Store or other distribution channels, understanding code signing, provisioning profiles, and the submission process is essential for a successful launch. By following best practices and conducting thorough testing, you can ensure a positive user experience for your app's users.

10.2. Navigating the App Store Connect

Once you've prepared your app for distribution and successfully submitted it for review on the App Store, you'll need to navigate the App Store Connect interface to manage your app's presence, monitor its performance, and interact with users and feedback. In this section, we'll explore the key features and functionalities of App Store Connect.

App Dashboard

Upon logging into App Store Connect[3], you'll be presented with the App Store Connect dashboard. This is your central hub for managing all aspects of your app's presence on the App Store. Here's what you'll find on the dashboard:

- **My Apps:** A list of all the apps associated with your developer account. Click on an app to access its details.

- **App Analytics:** Insights into your app's performance, including downloads, revenue, user engagement, and more.

- **Sales and Trends:** Detailed sales reports, including daily and weekly summaries, subscription data, and more.

- **Users and Access:** Manage user roles and permissions for your team working on the app.

- **Payments and Financial Reports:** View your financial data, earnings, and access financial reports.

---

3. https://appstoreconnect.apple.com/

- **Resources and Help:** Links to various resources and support for developers.

Managing Your App

Clicking on an app's name in the "My Apps" section takes you to the app's management page. Here, you can perform various actions:

- **App Information:** Edit and update your app's name, description, keywords, icon, screenshots, and other metadata.

- **Pricing and Availability:** Set the price of your app, choose the countries or regions where it's available, and configure pricing tiers.

- **In-App Purchases:** Create and manage in-app purchases for your app, including consumables, non-consumables, subscriptions, and more.

- **App Store Optimization (ASO):** Optimize your app's visibility on the App Store by improving keywords, title, and screenshots.

- **App Privacy:** Provide information about your app's data collection practices and privacy policies.

- **App Store Promotions:** Schedule promotional periods for your app or offer limited-time discounts.

- **App Store Page:** Preview how your app appears to users on the App Store and make adjustments as needed.

- **App Review:** Track the status of your app's review process and communicate with Apple's review team if necessary.

- **App Store Connect API:** Automate tasks and integrate with your development workflow using the API.

App Analytics

App Store Connect offers robust analytics tools to help you gain insights into your app's performance. Here are some key features:

- **Overview:** Get an overview of your app's downloads, sales, and active devices.

- **App Store Impressions:** See how often your app's product page was viewed on the App Store.

- **App Units:** Track the number of app units (downloads) and sales.

- **Sales and Trends:** Analyze your app's sales data, including revenue, subscriptions, and country-specific information.

- **App Analytics API:** Access analytics data programmatically to create custom reports or integrate with other tools.

User and Access Management

If you're working with a team of developers, designers, and marketers, you can manage their access to App Store Connect. Here's what you can do:

- **User Roles:** Assign different roles to team members, such as Admin, Developer, Marketer, and more, with varying levels of access and permissions.

- **Team Members:** Add team members to your development team and specify their roles.

- **Access Control:** Control who can perform specific actions, such as submitting apps for review or managing in-app purchases.

- **App-Specific Roles:** Assign team members specific roles for individual apps, allowing fine-grained control.

App Reviews and User Feedback

Monitoring user reviews and feedback is crucial for maintaining a positive app experience. Here's how to manage this aspect:

- **App Ratings and Reviews:** View and respond to user reviews on the App Store to address issues, provide support, and engage with your audience.

- **Feedback and Support:** Offer a way for users to contact your support team or provide feedback within the app.

- **App Store Connect API:** Automate the process of aggregating and analyzing user reviews and feedback.

Resources and Help

App Store Connect provides access to various resources to help you throughout the app development and distribution process:

- **Documentation:** Access detailed documentation and guides on various topics, from app submission to analytics.

- **Support and Contact:** Reach out to Apple's developer support team for assistance with specific issues or questions.

- **Forums and Communities:** Participate in developer forums and communities to connect with other developers and share insights.

- **News and Updates:** Stay informed about the latest news, updates, and announcements related to app development and distribution.

Conclusion

Navigating App Store Connect is essential for managing your app's presence on the App Store effectively. By understanding the dashboard, app management features, analytics tools, user and access control, and user feedback management, you can ensure your app's success and provide a positive experience for your users. Continuously monitoring and optimizing your app's performance and engagement will contribute to its long-term success in the App Store.

10.3. Understanding App Store Guidelines

As an app developer, it's crucial to understand and adhere to the App Store guidelines set by Apple. These guidelines ensure a consistent and high-quality experience for users and help maintain the integrity of the App Store ecosystem. In this section, we'll explore the key aspects of these guidelines.

Review Guidelines

Apple's App Store Review Guidelines outline the criteria your app must meet to be accepted and remain on the App Store. Here are some important points to consider:

- **Safety and Privacy:** Apps must not compromise user safety or violate privacy. This includes protecting user data and adhering to security best practices.

- **Content and Functionality:** Your app's content should be appropriate for all age groups, and it must function as intended without bugs or crashes.

- **Legal and Ethical Compliance:** Apps must comply with all applicable laws and regulations. This includes respecting copyright, trademark, and intellectual property rights.

- **User Interface:** Apps should have a clean and intuitive user interface. They should not mimic the iOS or Apple apps' design elements.

- **Performance:** Apps should be responsive, perform well, and not consume excessive battery life or data.

- **App Store Metadata:** The information provided about your app on the App Store, including its name, description, and screenshots, should be accurate and relevant.

- **Monetization:** If your app offers in-app purchases or subscriptions, it should clearly communicate the terms and pricing to users. Deceptive or hidden costs are not allowed.

- **App Store Conduct:** Developers are expected to conduct themselves professionally and not engage in fraudulent activities, such as fake reviews or click fraud.

App Store Review Process

When you submit your app to the App Store, it undergoes a review process conducted by Apple's review team. The team assesses whether your app complies with the guidelines and provides feedback or rejection if issues are identified.

Here's what you can expect during the review process:

- **Review Time:** The review time can vary but typically takes a few days. It's essential to factor in this time when planning app releases or updates.

- **Communication:** You can communicate with the review team through the App Store Connect interface if you have questions or need clarification.

- **Rejection and Appeals:** If your app is rejected, you'll receive feedback explaining the reasons. You can address the issues and resubmit your app for review.

- **App Updates:** Updates to your app also go through the review process to ensure they meet the latest guidelines.

Common Reasons for Rejection

To avoid app rejection, it's crucial to be aware of common reasons why apps get rejected during the review process. Here are some common issues:

- **Bugs and Crashes:** Apps that consistently crash or have major functionality issues will be rejected.

- **Inaccurate Information:** Providing incorrect or misleading information about your app can lead to rejection.

- **Incomplete Content:** Apps with placeholder content, incomplete features, or broken links are likely to be rejected.

- **Violations of Privacy:** Apps that collect user data without consent or fail to provide a privacy policy can be rejected.

- **Inappropriate Content:** Apps with explicit, offensive, or inappropriate content may be rejected.

- **Misleading Claims:** Making false claims about your app's features or functionality can result in rejection.

- **Use of Private APIs:** Accessing private APIs or using unauthorized frameworks can lead to rejection.

App Store Updates and Enforcement

Apple periodically updates the App Store guidelines, so it's essential to stay informed about any changes. Additionally, Apple enforces these guidelines and may remove apps from the App Store if they violate the rules. Developers are responsible for ensuring their apps remain compliant.

Conclusion

Understanding and adhering to the App Store guidelines is essential for app developers. By following these guidelines, you can increase the chances of your app being accepted and maintaining a positive presence on the App Store. Regularly reviewing the guidelines, addressing common rejection reasons, and ensuring your app complies with the rules will help you succeed in the iOS app ecosystem.

10.4. Marketing and Promoting Your App

Creating a great app is just the first step; you also need to effectively market and promote it to reach your target audience. In this section, we'll explore various strategies and techniques to help you promote your iOS app successfully.

1. App Store Optimization (ASO)

ASO is the process of optimizing your app's visibility on the App Store. Here are some key ASO strategies:

- **Keyword Optimization:** Choose relevant keywords for your app's title and description to improve discoverability.

- **Compelling Icon and Screenshots:** Design an eye-catching app icon and include high-quality screenshots that showcase your app's features.

- **Engaging Description:** Write a compelling and concise app description that highlights its unique selling points.

- **User Reviews and Ratings:** Encourage users to leave positive reviews and ratings, as these can influence others' decisions to download your app.

2. Social Media Marketing

Utilize popular social media platforms to create a presence for your app. Share updates, engage with your audience, and run targeted ad campaigns to reach potential users.

3. Influencer Marketing

Partner with influencers in your app's niche or industry to promote your app. Influencers can provide authentic reviews and demonstrations, which can be highly effective in driving downloads.

4. Content Marketing

Create valuable content related to your app's niche. This can include blog posts, videos, or podcasts. Share this content on your website and social media to attract and engage users.

5. Email Marketing

Build an email list of users interested in your app or industry. Send regular updates, newsletters, and promotional offers to keep them engaged and informed.

6. App Preview Videos

Create a captivating app preview video that showcases your app's key features and functionality. This can significantly impact users' decisions to download your app.

7. App Store Advertising

Consider running paid advertising campaigns within the App Store to increase visibility. Apple Search Ads allows you to target specific keywords and demographics.

8. Press Releases

Write and distribute press releases to relevant media outlets and tech blogs. Getting featured in reputable publications can boost your app's credibility.

9. App Launch Events

Organize an official launch event for your app, either virtually or in person. Use this opportunity to create buzz and attract attention from potential users and the media.

10. App Updates and Maintenance

Regularly update your app with new features, improvements, and bug fixes. This shows that you are committed to providing a great user experience and can lead to more positive reviews.

11. App Analytics

Use analytics tools to track user behavior, engagement, and retention. Analyze the data to make informed decisions and refine your marketing strategies.

12. User Feedback and Support

Listen to user feedback and respond promptly. Address issues and provide excellent customer support to maintain a positive reputation.

13. Cross-Promotion

Collaborate with other app developers for cross-promotion. Promote each other's apps to expand your user base.

14. Paid User Acquisition

Consider paid user acquisition campaigns through platforms like Facebook Ads, Google Ads, or ad networks specialized in mobile apps.

15. Localization

Localize your app by translating it into multiple languages to reach a broader global audience.

Remember that successful app promotion often requires a combination of these strategies. It's essential to monitor the effectiveness of your efforts and adapt your marketing approach as needed. Building and maintaining a strong online presence, engaging with your audience, and providing a valuable user experience are key to promoting your iOS app effectively.

10.5. Managing Feedback and Updates

Receiving feedback from your app's users is a valuable source of information for improving your app and keeping it up to date. In this section, we'll explore how to effectively manage user feedback and release updates for your iOS app.

1. Feedback Channels

Create accessible channels for users to provide feedback and report issues within your app. Common feedback channels include in-app forms, email support, and dedicated feedback sections. Encourage users to share their thoughts, report bugs, and suggest improvements.

2. User Surveys

Periodically conduct user surveys to gather specific feedback on features, user interface changes, or other aspects of your app. Surveys can provide valuable insights into user preferences and pain points.

3. App Store Reviews

Monitor and respond to user reviews on the App Store. Address concerns, thank users for positive feedback, and demonstrate your commitment to improving the app. Timely and respectful responses can enhance your app's reputation.

4. Bug Tracking and Issue Management

Use bug tracking tools like Jira, Trello, or GitHub Issues to efficiently manage reported bugs and feature requests. Categorize and prioritize issues to focus on critical improvements first.

5. Release Regular Updates

Frequent updates not only keep your app relevant but also show users that you are actively maintaining it. Include bug fixes, performance improvements, and new features in your updates.

6. Release Notes

Provide clear and informative release notes with each app update. Describe what has changed, what issues have been addressed, and what new features users can expect. Transparency builds trust with your audience.

7. Beta Testing

Before releasing major updates, consider conducting beta testing with a group of trusted users. Beta testers can provide valuable insights and help identify potential issues before the public release.

8. Versioning

Use a clear versioning system to indicate the significance of updates. For example, major updates could be labeled as "1.0," "2.0," while minor updates or bug fixes could use decimals like "1.1" or "1.2."

9. A/B Testing

Experiment with A/B testing to evaluate the impact of different app features, designs, or user interface changes. Data-driven decisions can lead to better user experiences.

10. Changelogs

Maintain a detailed changelog that lists all changes made in each app update. Changelogs help users understand what to expect in the latest version.

11. Continuous Improvement

Use the feedback received from users to drive continuous improvement. Actively address reported issues, implement feature requests when feasible, and iterate on your app's design and functionality.

12. User Communication

Keep users informed about upcoming updates and improvements through in-app notifications, email newsletters, or social media announcements. Engaging users in the update process can generate excitement and anticipation.

13. Compatibility Testing

Ensure that updates are compatible with various iOS versions and devices. Test your app thoroughly to avoid causing issues for users on older devices or operating systems.

14. App Store Guidelines

Always adhere to Apple's App Store guidelines when making updates. Non-compliance can lead to app rejection or removal from the App Store.

15. User Appreciation

Show appreciation to your loyal users by occasionally offering exclusive benefits, discounts, or promotions. Recognizing and rewarding user loyalty can foster a positive relationship.

Managing feedback and updates is an ongoing process that demonstrates your commitment to delivering a high-quality iOS app. By actively listening to your users and continuously improving your app based on their input, you can maintain a satisfied user base and ensure the long-term success of your app.

Chapter 11: Leveraging Frameworks and Libraries

Section 11.1: Exploring Apple's Frameworks

Apple's iOS development ecosystem provides developers with a rich set of frameworks that streamline app development and enhance functionality. These frameworks cover a wide range of domains, from user interface design to hardware interaction. In this section, we will explore some of the key Apple frameworks that can significantly impact your iOS app development process.

UIKit Framework

The UIKit framework is the cornerstone of iOS app development. It provides a set of classes and tools for creating user interfaces, managing user interactions, and handling app navigation. UIKit includes classes like UIViewController, UIButton, UILabel, and many more, making it easier to build visually appealing and responsive user interfaces.

```swift
import UIKit

class MyViewController: UIViewController {

override func viewDidLoad() {

super.viewDidLoad()

let button = UIButton(type: .system)

button.setTitle("Click Me", for: .normal)

button.addTarget(self, action: #selector(buttonClicked), for: .touchUpInside)

view.addSubview(button)

}

@objc func buttonClicked() {

// Handle button click here
```

```
}

}
```

Core Data Framework

Core Data is Apple's persistence framework that simplifies data management within your app. It allows you to define data models, create, retrieve, update, and delete records in a database-like manner. Core Data is excellent for managing local data storage, including user preferences, cached content, and more.

```
import CoreData

// Create a managed object context

let context = persistentContainer.viewContext

// Create a new managed object

if          let          entityDescription          =
NSEntityDescription.entity(forEntityName: "Person", in: context) {

let person = NSManagedObject(entity: entityDescription,
insertInto: context)

person.setValue("John Doe", forKey: "name")

}

// Save changes to the persistent store

do {

try context.save()

} catch {
```

```
print("Error saving context: \(error)")
```

```
}
```

MapKit Framework

MapKit provides developers with tools for integrating interactive maps and location-based services into their applications. With MapKit, you can display maps, add annotations, calculate routes, and utilize the user's location. It's widely used in apps that require mapping and navigation features.

import MapKit

```
let mapView = MKMapView(frame: CGRect(x: 0, y: 0, width: 300, height: 300))
```

```
let location = CLLocationCoordinate2D(latitude: 37.7749, longitude: -122.4194)
```

```
let region = MKCoordinateRegion(center: location, span: MKCoordinateSpan(latitudeDelta: 0.1, longitudeDelta: 0.1))
```

```
mapView.setRegion(region, animated: true)
```

```
let annotation = MKPointAnnotation()
```

```
annotation.coordinate = location
```

```
annotation.title = "San Francisco"
```

```
mapView.addAnnotation(annotation)
```

AVFoundation Framework

The AVFoundation framework enables multimedia-related functionality in your app. It allows you to work with audio and video, capture media from the camera and microphone, and perform various media manipulations. AVFoundation is crucial for building apps that involve multimedia content.

import AVFoundation

let audioPlayer = **try?** AVAudioPlayer(contentsOf: audioURL)

audioPlayer?.play()

let captureSession = AVCaptureSession()

if let captureDevice = AVCaptureDevice.**default**(**for**: .video),

let input = **try?** AVCaptureDeviceInput(device: captureDevice) {

if captureSession.canAddInput(input) {

captureSession.addInput(input)

}

}

SwiftUI Framework

SwiftUI is a relatively new framework that simplifies the creation of user interfaces with a declarative syntax. It allows you to build user interfaces for iOS, macOS, watchOS, and tvOS using the same codebase. SwiftUI provides a modern and efficient way to design app interfaces.

```swift
import SwiftUI

struct ContentView: View {

var body: some View {

Text("Hello, SwiftUI!")

.font(.largeTitle)

.foregroundColor(.blue)

}

}

@main

struct MyApp: App {

var body: some Scene {

WindowGroup {

ContentView()

}

}

}
```

These are just a few examples of the many Apple frameworks available for iOS development. Exploring and utilizing these frameworks can greatly enhance the capabilities and user experience of your iOS apps. In the following sections, we'll delve into integrating third-party libraries and frameworks to expand your app's functionality further.

Section 11.2: Integrating Third-Party Libraries

In the world of iOS development, you don't have to build everything from scratch. There is a vast ecosystem of third-party libraries and frameworks created by other developers and communities that can help you save time and effort. These libraries cover a wide range of functionalities, from networking and data persistence to UI components and animations. Integrating third-party libraries into your project can significantly speed up development and bring advanced features to your app.

The CocoaPods Dependency Manager

One of the most popular tools for managing third-party libraries in iOS projects is CocoaPods. CocoaPods is a dependency manager that simplifies the process of adding and updating external libraries. To get started with CocoaPods, you need to have Ruby installed on your system. Here's how you can integrate CocoaPods into your project:

1. Install CocoaPods using the terminal:

sudo gem install cocoapods

1. Navigate to your Xcode project directory and create a Podfile:

cd /path/to/your/project

touch Podfile

1. Edit the Podfile to specify the libraries you want to use. For example, if you want to add the popular Alamofire library

for networking:

```
platform :ios, '14.0'
```

```
use_frameworks!
```

```
target 'YourApp' do
```

```
pod 'Alamofire', '~> 5.0'
```

```
end
```

Replace 'YourApp' with the name of your Xcode target.

1. Install the specified libraries by running:

```
pod install
```

1. Close your Xcode project and open the newly created .xcworkspace file. This workspace includes your project and the CocoaPods dependencies.
2. Now, you can import and use the third-party libraries in your Swift code as needed.

Carthage: Another Dependency Manager

Carthage is another popular dependency manager for iOS projects, and it offers a different approach compared to CocoaPods. Carthage focuses on binary frameworks, which means it compiles and manages pre-built libraries instead of distributing source code. Here's how to use Carthage:

1. Install Carthage using Homebrew:

```
brew install carthage
```

1. Create a Cartfile in your project directory:

cd /path/to/your/project

touch Cartfile

1. Edit the Cartfile to specify the libraries you want to include. For example, to add the popular Kingfisher library for image downloading and caching:

github "onevcat/Kingfisher" ~> 7.0

1. Fetch and build the libraries by running:

carthage update

1. Follow the instructions provided by Carthage to integrate the built frameworks into your Xcode project.

Both CocoaPods and Carthage have their advantages and trade-offs. CocoaPods provides a more straightforward setup process and supports dynamic frameworks. Carthage, on the other hand, focuses on simplicity and avoids some of the complexity introduced by CocoaPods. Your choice of dependency manager may depend on your project's specific requirements and your personal preferences.

Guidelines for Using Third-Party Libraries

While third-party libraries can be incredibly helpful, it's essential to use them judiciously and consider the following guidelines:

1. **Check Compatibility**: Ensure that the library is compatible with the version of Swift and iOS you're using. Outdated libraries may cause compatibility issues.

2. **Community and Support**: Choose libraries with an active community and regular updates. This ensures that issues are addressed, and the library remains up to date.

3. **License Compliance**: Review the library's license to ensure it aligns with your project's licensing requirements. Some libraries may have restrictions on commercial use.

4. **Security**: Be cautious when including libraries that perform critical functions, such as authentication or encryption. Security vulnerabilities in third-party code can have serious consequences.

5. **Documentation**: A well-documented library is easier to integrate and maintain. Look for libraries with clear documentation and usage examples.

6. **Performance Impact**: Consider the performance impact of adding a library. Some libraries may introduce overhead or bloat that affects your app's performance.

7. **Keep Dependencies Minimal**: Avoid adding too many dependencies to your project. Over-reliance on third-party code can complicate maintenance and increase the risk of compatibility issues.

By following these guidelines and making informed choices, you can harness the power of third-party libraries to enhance your iOS app development while maintaining code quality and reliability.

Section 11.3: Using CocoaPods and Carthage

In this section, we will delve deeper into the practical aspects of using CocoaPods and Carthage as dependency managers for your iOS projects. Both tools are immensely valuable for managing third-party libraries, but they have different workflows and offer distinct advantages.

CocoaPods Workflow

CocoaPods streamlines the process of adding and updating third-party libraries to your Xcode project. Follow these steps to use CocoaPods effectively:

1. **Initialize CocoaPods**: Before you can use CocoaPods in your project, you need to initialize it. Open your terminal and navigate to your project's root directory. Then, run the following command:

```
pod init
```

This will create a Podfile in your project directory.

1. **Edit Your Podfile**: Open the newly created Podfile in a text editor and specify the libraries you want to add. Here's an example Podfile:

```
platform :ios, '15.0'

use_frameworks!

target 'YourApp' do

pod 'Alamofire', '~> 5.0'

pod 'SwiftyJSON', '~> 4.0'

end
```

Replace 'YourApp' with your project's target name. The platform line specifies the minimum iOS version required.

1. **Install Dependencies**: Save the Podfile and return to your terminal. Run the following command to install the specified dependencies:

pod install

CocoaPods will download the libraries and create a .xcworkspace file for your project.

1. **Open Workspace**: From now on, always open your Xcode project using the .xcworkspace file. This workspace includes your project and the CocoaPods dependencies.
2. **Use Imported Libraries**: You can now import and use the third-party libraries in your Swift code as needed. Xcode will automatically provide code completion for the imported modules.
3. **Update Dependencies**: Periodically, check for updates to your dependencies by running:

pod update

This command updates the libraries to their latest compatible versions.

Carthage Workflow

Carthage offers an alternative approach to managing dependencies by focusing on binary frameworks. Here's how to use Carthage effectively:

1. **Install Carthage**: If you haven't already, install Carthage using Homebrew with the following command:

brew install carthage

1. **Create Cartfile**: In your project directory, create a Cartfile that lists the libraries you want to include. For example:

github "Alamofire/Alamofire" ~> 5.0

github "SwiftyJSON/SwiftyJSON" ~> 4.0

Specify the GitHub repository and the desired version.

1. **Fetch Dependencies**: Fetch and build the dependencies by running:

carthage update

Carthage will download and compile the libraries into a Carthage/Build directory.

1. **Integrate Frameworks**: In Xcode, go to your project settings and select your target. Under the "General" tab, add the frameworks from the Carthage/Build/iOS directory to the "Frameworks, Libraries, and Embedded Content" section.
2. **Run Scripts**: To ensure that Carthage-built frameworks are properly copied to your app's bundle during the build process, add a "Run Script" phase in your target's build phases with the following command:

/usr/local/bin/carthage copy-frameworks

In the "Input Files" section, add the paths to the frameworks you want to copy, like this:

$(SRCROOT)/Carthage/Build/iOS/
Alamofire.framework

$(SRCROOT)/Carthage/Build/iOS/
SwiftyJSON.framework

This script will ensure that the frameworks are available when you run your app.

Both CocoaPods and Carthage are excellent tools for dependency management in iOS projects, and your choice between them may depend on your project's specific needs and your familiarity with the workflow.

Pros and Cons

- **CocoaPods Pros**:

- Simple setup and integration.

- Manages both source code and binary frameworks.

- Offers a centralized repository of libraries (CocoaPods Trunk).

- Extensive community support and a wide selection of libraries.

- **CocoaPods Cons**:

- Can lead to complex project structures when managing multiple dependencies.

- Version conflicts between libraries can occur.

- **Carthage Pros**:

- Focuses on binary frameworks, reducing project bloat.

– Promotes cleaner project structures.

– Allows you to specify dependencies by their GitHub repository, which can simplify library selection.

• **Carthage Cons**:

– Requires manual integration of frameworks.

– No centralized repository, so you must rely on GitHub or other hosting services.

Ultimately, the choice between CocoaPods and Carthage depends on your project's specific needs and your personal preferences

Section 11.4: Building Custom Frameworks

In this section, we'll explore the process of creating custom frameworks in Xcode. Custom frameworks are a powerful way to modularize and encapsulate code for reuse across multiple projects. They allow you to create a set of functionalities that can be easily added to any iOS application, enhancing code maintainability and reusability.

Creating a Custom Framework

Follow these steps to create a custom framework in Xcode:

1. **Create a New Project**: Open Xcode and create a new project. Select the "iOS Framework" template under the "Framework & Library" section.
2. **Configure Your Framework**: Name your framework and specify its organization identifier. Choose the language (usually Swift) and set the destination to "iOS." Click

"Next" and choose a location for your project.

3. **Add Code**: Within your framework project, create Swift files and add the code that defines the functionality you want to encapsulate. For example, if you're building a networking framework, you might define networking operations and API endpoints.

4. **Build Your Framework**: Build the framework by selecting a target (e.g., "MyFramework") and running the build process. This generates a .framework file in the "Products" group of your project.

5. **Use the Framework**: To use your custom framework in another project, you can either copy the .framework file manually or use a dependency manager like CocoaPods or Carthage, as discussed in previous sections. Make sure to add the framework to the "Frameworks, Libraries, and Embedded Content" section of your target's settings.

6. **Import and Use**: In the project where you want to use the custom framework, import it using import MyFramework. You can then access the functionality provided by the framework's APIs.

Framework Best Practices

Here are some best practices to follow when creating custom frameworks:

- **Modularization**: Divide your framework into well-organized modules or components, each responsible for a specific set of functionalities. This promotes clean code and makes it easier to understand and maintain.

- **Versioning**: Implement versioning for your framework to ensure compatibility with different versions of client projects. Semantic versioning (e.g., 1.0.0) is a widely accepted practice.

● **Documentation**: Provide comprehensive documentation for your framework, including clear explanations of how to use it, code examples, and information about the available APIs. Tools like Jazzy can generate documentation from your code.

● **Testing**: Write unit tests for your framework to ensure its reliability and correctness. Consider using the framework in test projects to catch any issues.

● **Continuous Integration**: Set up continuous integration (CI) pipelines to build, test, and deploy your framework automatically. CI tools like Travis CI or GitHub Actions can be helpful.

● **Error Handling**: Implement robust error handling mechanisms within your framework, and document error codes and error messages for users to understand issues they might encounter.

● **Dependencies**: Be mindful of dependencies your framework relies on. Document these dependencies and their versions, and ensure they are well-maintained.

Framework Distribution

When distributing your custom framework, you have several options:

1. **Private Distribution**: You can keep the framework private and use it only within your organization's projects. In this

case, you can distribute it via a private Git repository or a shared file system.

2. **Public Distribution**: If you want to share your framework with a broader audience, consider publishing it on a platform like GitHub as an open-source project. This allows others to contribute, report issues, and use your framework.

3. **Package Managers**: You can also distribute your framework using dependency managers like CocoaPods or Carthage, making it easy for other developers to integrate it into their projects.

Remember to adhere to licensing and legal considerations when distributing your framework, especially if it includes third-party code or libraries.

Creating custom frameworks in Xcode empowers you to encapsulate and share your code effectively, enhancing the maintainability and reusability of your iOS projects. By following best practices and making your framework well-documented and modular, you can contribute valuable tools to the iOS development community and streamline your own app development processes.

Section 11.5: Cross-Platform Development with SwiftUI

In this section, we'll delve into cross-platform development with SwiftUI, Apple's modern UI framework that allows you to build user interfaces for iOS, macOS, watchOS, and tvOS using a single codebase. SwiftUI simplifies the process of creating responsive and native-like interfaces across various Apple platforms.

Introduction to SwiftUI

SwiftUI is a declarative UI framework, meaning you describe the user interface's structure and behavior, and SwiftUI takes care of rendering it appropriately on different devices and orientations. It offers a wide range of UI elements, layout options, and animations, making it a powerful choice for cross-platform development.

Building a Cross-Platform App

To create a cross-platform app with SwiftUI, follow these steps:

1. **Create a New Project**: Open Xcode and create a new project, selecting the "App" template. Choose a project name and make sure the "Use SwiftUI" checkbox is selected.

2. **Define Your Views**: SwiftUI relies on views and modifiers to construct user interfaces. You'll define your app's views using SwiftUI's syntax. Views can include buttons, text fields, lists, and more.

3. **Organize Your Code**: SwiftUI promotes a modular approach to app development. Organize your code into separate views and structs for better readability and maintainability.

4. **Adaptive Layout**: SwiftUI provides tools for creating adaptive layouts that adjust to different screen sizes and orientations. You can use stacks, grids, and alignment guides to control the layout.

5. **Preview Your App**: One of SwiftUI's advantages is its live preview feature, which allows you to see your app's UI changes in real-time as you make edits to your code. This accelerates the development and debugging process.

6. **Test Across Platforms**: You can run and test your app on

different Apple platforms like iOS, macOS, watchOS, and tvOS by choosing the appropriate device simulator in Xcode.

Platform-Specific Code

While SwiftUI is cross-platform, there may be instances where you need to write platform-specific code. SwiftUI provides the @available attribute to conditionally include or exclude code based on the target platform. For example:

```
@available(iOS 15, *)

struct iOSView: View {

var body: some View {

Text("This is iOS-specific code.")

}

}

@available(macOS 12, *)

struct macOSView: View {

var body: some View {

Text("This is macOS-specific code.")

}

}
```

In this example, the iOSView will be available on iOS 15 or later, while the macOSView is available on macOS 12 or later. This allows you to customize the user experience for different platforms while sharing most of the codebase.

Limitations and Considerations

While SwiftUI offers many advantages for cross-platform development, there are some limitations and considerations to keep in mind:

- **Platform Availability**: Not all SwiftUI features are available on every platform. Check Apple's documentation for platform-specific features and limitations.

- **User Interface Differences**: Each platform has its own design guidelines and user interface paradigms. While SwiftUI handles many of these differences, you may need to customize your UI for each platform to provide the best user experience.

- **Performance**: Performance may vary between platforms, especially on devices with different hardware capabilities. Profile and optimize your app for each target platform.

- **App Store Guidelines**: Be aware of the guidelines and requirements for each platform's app store when distributing your app.

- **Third-Party Libraries**: Check the availability of third-party libraries and dependencies for each platform. Some libraries may not be compatible with all platforms.

In conclusion, SwiftUI is a powerful tool for cross-platform development on Apple's ecosystem. With a single codebase, you can target multiple platforms, reducing development time and effort. However, it's essential to be mindful of platform-specific differences and optimize your app for each target to provide the best user experience.

Chapter 12: Advanced Swift Programming

Section 12.1: Functional Programming in Swift

Functional programming is a programming paradigm that treats computation as the evaluation of mathematical functions and avoids changing state and mutable data. Swift is a multi-paradigm language that supports functional programming, making it possible to write clean, concise, and expressive code. In this section, we'll explore key functional programming concepts in Swift.

1. First-Class and Higher-Order Functions

In Swift, functions are first-class citizens, meaning you can assign them to variables, pass them as arguments to other functions, and return them from functions. This feature allows you to write higher-order functions, which are functions that take other functions as parameters or return them as results.

Here's an example of a simple higher-order function that applies a given function to each element of an array and returns a new array:

```swift
func applyOperation(_ numbers: [Int], _ operation: (Int) -> Int) -> [Int] {

var result = [Int]()

for number in numbers {

result.append(operation(number))

}
```

```swift
return result
}

let numbers = [1, 2, 3, 4, 5]

let squaredNumbers = applyOperation(numbers) { $0 * $0 }

print(squaredNumbers) // Output: [1, 4, 9, 16, 25]
```

In this example, the applyOperation function takes an array of integers and a closure (function) as parameters. It applies the closure to each element of the array and returns a new array containing the results.

2. Map, Filter, and Reduce

Swift provides built-in higher-order functions like map, filter, and reduce that simplify common functional programming tasks:

- map: Transforms each element of an array using a given transformation function and returns a new array with the transformed values.

```swift
let numbers = [1, 2, 3, 4, 5]

let squaredNumbers = numbers.map { $0 * $0 }

print(squaredNumbers) // Output: [1, 4, 9, 16, 25]
```

- filter: Filters the elements of an array based on a given condition and returns a new array containing the filtered elements.

```swift
let numbers = [1, 2, 3, 4, 5]

let evenNumbers = numbers.filter { $0 % 2 == 0 }
```

```
print(evenNumbers) // Output: [2, 4]
```

- reduce: Combines all elements of an array into a single value using a given combining function.

```
let numbers = [1, 2, 3, 4, 5]

let sum = numbers.reduce(0) { $0 + $1 }

print(sum) // Output: 15
```

These functions promote immutability and expressiveness in your code.

3. Closures and Capture Lists

Closures are self-contained blocks of functionality that can be passed around and used in your code. They capture and store references to any constants and variables from the surrounding context in which they are defined. To prevent strong reference cycles, you can use capture lists to specify how closures capture and store references.

```
class MyViewController {

var data: [String] = ["A", "B", "C"]

func configureClosure() {

let closure: () -> Void = { [weak self] in

self?.data.append("D")

print(self?.data ?? [])

}

closure()
```

```
}

}
```

In this example, we use a capture list [weak self] to capture self weakly within the closure, preventing a strong reference cycle.

4. Functional Composition

Functional programming encourages composing small, reusable functions to build more complex ones. Swift provides a composition operator (<<<) that allows you to combine functions to create new functions.

```
func addOne(_ x: Int) -> Int {

return x + 1

}

func double(_ x: Int) -> Int {

return x * 2

}

let transform = addOne <<< double

let result = transform(5) // Equivalent to addOne(double(5))

print(result) // Output: 11
```

Conclusion

Functional programming concepts in Swift, such as first-class functions, higher-order functions, and immutability, enable you to write more modular, maintainable, and expressive code.

Understanding these concepts can lead to cleaner and more efficient Swift code.

Section 12.2: Concurrency and Parallel Programming

Concurrency and parallel programming are essential in modern software development to efficiently utilize multiple CPU cores and provide responsive user experiences. Swift provides several mechanisms and APIs to work with concurrency and parallelism. In this section, we'll explore key concepts and tools for concurrent and parallel programming in Swift.

1. DispatchQueue and Asynchronous Tasks

Swift's DispatchQueue is a powerful tool for managing concurrency. It allows you to dispatch tasks to run concurrently or asynchronously on different threads. You can use DispatchQueue to offload time-consuming tasks from the main thread, ensuring that your app remains responsive.

Here's an example of using DispatchQueue to perform a task asynchronously:

```swift
let queue = DispatchQueue(label: "com.example.myqueue")

queue.async {

// Perform a time-consuming task

for i in 1...5 {

print("Task \(i)")

}
```

```
}
```

In this example, a custom queue is created, and a task is dispatched asynchronously to run on that queue. This keeps the main thread free to handle user interface updates.

2. Dispatch Groups

DispatchGroup allows you to group multiple tasks and wait for all of them to complete before proceeding. This is useful when you have several concurrent tasks and want to perform some action only after all of them finish.

```swift
let group = DispatchGroup()

for i in 1...3 {

group.enter()

DispatchQueue.global().async {

// Perform a task

print("Task \(i) completed")

group.leave()

}

}

group.notify(queue: .main) {

// This block is executed when all tasks are completed

print("All tasks completed")

}
```

In this example, tasks are entered into the group before they are dispatched. The group.notify block executes when all tasks in the group have completed.

3. Swift Concurrency Model

Starting with Swift 5.5, a new concurrency model was introduced, which includes the async and await keywords. This model simplifies asynchronous programming by allowing you to write asynchronous code in a more synchronous style.

```swift
func fetchUserData() async -> User {

// Perform asynchronous operation

let data = await fetchData()

let user = try await parseUserData(data)

return user

}

Task {

do {

let user = try await fetchUserData()

print("User data fetched: \(user)")

} catch {

print("Error fetching user data: \(error)")

}

}
```

In this example, the async and await keywords make it clear which parts of the code are asynchronous. The Task API is used to run asynchronous code in a structured way.

4. Parallelism with Swift

Swift also provides facilities for parallel programming using multiple CPU cores. You can use the parallelMap function to parallelize the processing of a collection.

let numbers = [1, 2, 3, 4, 5]

let doubledNumbers = numbers.parallelMap { $0 * 2 }

print(doubledNumbers) // *Output: [2, 4, 6, 8, 10]*

In this example, parallelMap distributes the work across multiple CPU cores, speeding up the processing of the array.

Conclusion

Concurrency and parallelism are critical for building responsive and efficient applications. Swift provides a range of tools and APIs, including DispatchQueue, DispatchGroup, and the Swift Concurrency Model, to help you manage and leverage concurrency effectively in your Swift projects. Understanding these concepts is essential for developing high-performance applications.

Section 12.3: Advanced Type System in Swift

Swift boasts a powerful and flexible type system, allowing developers to express complex relationships between types and write more robust and maintainable code. In this section, we'll delve into some advanced aspects of Swift's type system.

1. Generics

Generics in Swift enable you to write flexible, reusable code that works with different types. You can define functions, classes, and structures that operate on generic types without specifying the exact type they will work with until they are used. Here's a simple example of a generic function:

```swift
func swapTwoValues<T>(_ a: inout T, _ b: inout T) {

let temp = a

a = b

b = temp

}

var a = 5

var b = 10

swapTwoValues(&a, &b)

print("a: \(a), b: \(b)") // Output: a: 10, b: 5
```

In this example, swapTwoValues is a generic function that can swap values of any type.

2. Associated Types and Protocols

Swift protocols can include associated types, which allow protocols to describe types that conforming types must provide. This is particularly useful for abstracting away concrete types while still enforcing type safety. Here's an example using associated types in a protocol:

```swift
protocol Container {

associatedtype Item

mutating func append(_ item: Item)

var count: Int { get }

subscript(_ index: Int) -> Item { get }

}

struct Stack<Element>: Container {

typealias Item = Element

private var items: [Element] = []

mutating func append(_ item: Element) {

items.append(item)

}

var count: Int {

return items.count

}

subscript(_ index: Int) -> Element {

return items[index]

}

}

var stack = Stack<Int>()
```

stack.append(1)

stack.append(2)

print(stack[0]) // *Output: 1*

In this example, the Container protocol defines an associated type Item, and the Stack struct conforms to this protocol while specifying the associated type as Int.

3. Type Erasure

Type erasure is a technique used to hide the concrete types of objects while still providing a uniform interface. It's often used when dealing with protocols that have associated types. A common use case is to wrap objects of different types into a single type-erased container. Here's an example:

```swift
struct AnyContainer<T>: Container {

private var _append: (T) -> Void

private var _count: () -> Int

private var _subscript: (Int) -> T

init<C: Container>(_ container: C) where C.Item == T {

_append = { item in container.append(item) }

_count = { container.count }

_subscript = { index in container[index] }

}

mutating func append(_ item: T) {
```

```swift
_append(item)

}

var count: Int {

return _count()

}

subscript(_ index: Int) -> T {

return _subscript(index)

}

}

var anyStack = AnyContainer(Stack<Int>())

anyStack.append(3)

print(anyStack[0]) // Output: 3
```

In this example, AnyContainer is a type-erased container that wraps any type conforming to the Container protocol. It uses closures to delegate the operations to the wrapped container.

4. Advanced Type Constraints

Swift's type system allows you to define complex type constraints using where clauses. This enables you to specify requirements that types must satisfy when declaring generic functions or types. For example, you can constrain a generic type to conform to multiple protocols or specify that it must have a particular initializer.

```swift
func process<T: Equatable & CustomStringConvertible>(_ value:
T) {
```

```
print("Value: \(value), Description: \(value.description)")
}
```

```
process(42) // Output: Value: 42, Description: 42
```

In this example, the process function accepts a generic type T but constrains it to types that conform to both Equatable and CustomStringConvertible.

Conclusion

Swift's advanced type system, including generics, associated types, type erasure, and type constraints, empowers developers to write expressive and reusable code. Understanding these concepts is crucial for building maintainable and flexible software solutions in Swift.

Section 12.4: Protocol-Oriented Programming

Protocol-oriented programming (POP) is a paradigm in Swift that emphasizes the use of protocols to define the blueprint of functionality and structure in your code. It complements object-oriented programming (OOP) and enhances code reuse and composition. In this section, we'll explore the principles and advantages of POP.

1. Protocols as Blueprints

In POP, protocols serve as blueprints that define the methods, properties, and requirements that types conforming to the protocol must implement. By designing your code around protocols, you create clear and flexible contracts between different parts of your codebase.

```swift
protocol Animal {

var name: String { get }

func makeSound()

}

struct Dog: Animal {

let name: String

func makeSound() {

print("Woof!")

}

}

struct Cat: Animal {

let name: String

func makeSound() {

print("Meow!")

}

}
```

In this example, the Animal protocol defines a contract for types that represent animals. Both Dog and Cat conform to this protocol and provide their implementations.

2. Protocol Extensions

Protocol extensions allow you to provide default implementations for methods and properties defined in a protocol. This enables you to add functionality to existing types without modifying their source code. It's a powerful way to achieve code reusability and maintainability.

```swift
extension Animal {

func greet() {

print("Hello, I'm \(name)!")

}

}

let myDog = Dog(name: "Buddy")

myDog.greet() // Output: Hello, I'm Buddy!
```

Here, we've extended the Animal protocol with a greet() method, and all types conforming to Animal gain this functionality.

3. Protocol Composition

Protocol composition allows you to combine multiple protocols into a single, composite protocol. This is useful when you want to specify that a type should conform to multiple protocols at once.

```swift
protocol Swimmer {

func swim()

}

protocol Flyer {
```

```
func fly()

}

// A Bird that can both swim and fly

struct Bird: Swimmer, Flyer {

func swim() {

print("Bird swimming.")

}

func fly() {

print("Bird flying.")

}

}
```

In this example, Bird conforms to both Swimmer and Flyer protocols, and it implements the required methods for each.

4. Value Types and Immutability

POP encourages the use of value types (structs and enums) due to their immutability and thread safety. Value types align well with the principles of functional programming, allowing you to create predictable and side-effect-free code.

```
protocol Counter {

var count: Int { get }

mutating func increment()

}
```

```swift
struct CounterImpl: Counter {

private(set) var count: Int = 0

mutating func increment() {

count += 1

}

}

var counter = CounterImpl()

counter.increment()

print(counter.count) // Output: 1
```

Here, the Counter protocol defines a contract for counters, and the CounterImpl struct conforms to it. Value types ensure that changes are localized and don't affect other parts of the code.

5. Advantages of POP

- **Code Reusability**: Protocols and protocol extensions promote code reuse across different types.

- **Flexibility**: POP provides flexibility to add functionality to types without modifying their source code.

- **Composition**: Protocol composition allows you to specify complex requirements for types.

- **Value Types**: Embracing value types enhances code predictability and immutability.

- **Testability**: POP leads to code that is highly testable and easier to reason about.

In conclusion, protocol-oriented programming is a valuable approach in Swift development, promoting clear contracts, code reusability, and maintainability. By understanding and applying POP principles, you can write more robust and flexible code in your iOS and macOS applications.

Section 12.5: Leveraging Swift's Standard Library

Swift's Standard Library is a rich collection of data types, protocols, and functions that provide fundamental building blocks for your code. In this section, we'll explore some of the essential components of the Swift Standard Library and how to leverage them effectively in your iOS development.

1. Collections

Swift's Standard Library offers powerful collection types, including arrays, dictionaries, sets, and sequences, that are essential for managing and manipulating data.

```swift
// Array

var fruits = ["Apple", "Banana", "Orange"]

fruits.append("Mango")

print(fruits) // Output: ["Apple", "Banana", "Orange", "Mango"]

// Dictionary

var scores = ["Alice": 95, "Bob": 88, "Charlie": 92]
```

```swift
scores["David"] = 78

print(scores) // Output: ["Alice": 95, "Bob": 88, "Charlie": 92,
"David": 78]

// Set

var uniqueNumbers: Set<Int> = [1, 2, 3, 4, 5, 5]

print(uniqueNumbers) // Output: [5, 1, 2, 3, 4]

// Sequence

for number in 1...5 {

print(number)

}
```

2. Optionals

Swift's Standard Library introduced optionals to represent the absence of a value or the presence of a value that may be nil. Optionals help eliminate null pointer errors and make code more robust.

```swift
var temperature: Double? = 23.5 // Optional Double

if let temp = temperature {

print("Temperature is \(temp)°C")

} else {

print("Temperature is unknown")

}
```

3. Error Handling

Swift provides a robust error-handling mechanism using the Error protocol and throws keyword. You can throw and catch errors to handle exceptional cases gracefully.

```swift
enum NetworkError: Error {

case connectionLost

case serverError

}

func fetchData() throws {

// Simulate a network error

throw NetworkError.serverError

}

do {

try fetchData()

} catch NetworkError.connectionLost {

print("Connection lost")

} catch NetworkError.serverError {

print("Server error")

} catch {

print("Unknown error")

}
```

4. Functional Programming

Swift's Standard Library embraces functional programming concepts, offering functions like map, filter, and reduce to work with collections more elegantly.

```swift
let numbers = [1, 2, 3, 4, 5]

let doubled = numbers.map { $0 * 2 }

print(doubled) // Output: [2, 4, 6, 8, 10]

let evenNumbers = numbers.filter { $0 % 2 == 0 }

print(evenNumbers) // Output: [2, 4]

let sum = numbers.reduce(0, +)

print(sum) // Output: 15
```

5. String Manipulation

Swift's Standard Library provides powerful string manipulation capabilities, making it easier to work with text and perform operations like splitting, joining, and searching.

```swift
let sentence = "Swift is a powerful programming language."

let words = sentence.split(separator: " ")

print(words) // Output: ["Swift", "is", "a", "powerful", "programming", "language."]

let fruits = ["Apple", "Banana", "Orange"]

let fruitString = fruits.joined(separator: ", ")

print(fruitString) // Output: "Apple, Banana, Orange"
```

```swift
let greeting = "Hello, World!"

if greeting.contains("Hello") {

print("Found greeting")

}
```

6. Date and Time

Swift's Standard Library includes the Date struct for working with dates and times. You can perform various date calculations and formatting using this type.

```swift
let now = Date()

let dateFormatter = DateFormatter()

dateFormatter.dateFormat = "yyyy-MM-dd HH:mm:ss"

let formattedDate = dateFormatter.string(from: now)

print(formattedDate) // Output: "2024-01-22 15:30:00"
```

7. Conclusion

Swift's Standard Library is a valuable resource for iOS developers, offering a wide range of tools to simplify common tasks and improve code quality. By leveraging these standard components, you can write more efficient and maintainable iOS applications.

Chapter 13: Advanced Debugging Techniques

Section 13.1: Memory Management and Leaks

Memory management is a critical aspect of iOS development. Properly managing memory is essential to ensure that your app runs smoothly and doesn't consume more resources than necessary. In this section, we'll delve into memory management and memory leaks in iOS applications.

Understanding Memory Management

iOS uses Automatic Reference Counting (ARC) to manage memory. ARC automatically keeps track of how many references there are to a particular object and releases the memory when the object is no longer needed. While ARC simplifies memory management, you still need to be mindful of memory cycles and retain cycles that can lead to memory leaks.

Identifying Memory Leaks

Memory leaks occur when objects are not deallocated properly, leading to a gradual increase in memory usage. Identifying memory leaks can be challenging, but Xcode provides tools to help you diagnose and fix them.

Using Instruments

Instruments is a powerful profiling tool in Xcode that can help you find memory leaks. To use Instruments for memory analysis, follow these steps:

1. Open Xcode and go to "Product" > "Profile" > "Instruments."
2. Choose the "Leaks" instrument from the list.
3. Click the "Record" button to start profiling your app.
4. Interact with your app to trigger the code paths that you suspect might have memory leaks.
5. Instruments will highlight any memory leaks in your code, showing you where they occur.

Analyzing Leaks in Xcode

Xcode also has a built-in memory graph debugger that allows you to visualize object relationships and detect memory issues. To use the memory graph debugger:

1. Run your app in debug mode.
2. Open the Debug Navigator in Xcode.
3. Select the "Memory" tab.
4. Use the memory graph debugger to inspect object relationships and find potential retain cycles.

Fixing Memory Leaks

Once you've identified a memory leak, it's essential to fix it promptly. The most common causes of memory leaks are strong reference cycles, where objects reference each other, preventing them from being deallocated. To break such cycles, you can use one of the following approaches:

Use Weak References

In situations where you want to avoid strong reference cycles, use weak references. Weak references don't increase the reference count of an object, allowing it to be deallocated when no strong references exist.

```
class Person {

weak var spouse: Person?

}
```

Use Capture Lists

When working with closures, be cautious about creating retain cycles. You can use capture lists to specify how variables should be captured, helping to break retain cycles.

```
lazy var someClosure: () -> Void = { [weak self] in

self?.doSomething()

}
```

Use Unowned References

Unowned references are similar to weak references but assume that the reference will always have a value. Use unowned references when you know the referenced object will exist throughout the object's lifetime.

```swift
class Article {

unowned let author: Author

init(author: Author) {

self.author = author

}

}
```

Conclusion

Memory management is a crucial aspect of iOS development. Understanding how memory management works, identifying memory leaks, and adopting best practices for managing memory will help you create high-quality and performant iOS applications. Using the tools provided by Xcode, you can effectively detect and resolve memory issues, ensuring that your app runs smoothly for your users.

Section 13.2: Advanced Breakpoints and Watchpoints

In iOS development, debugging is an essential part of the development process. While Xcode provides a range of debugging tools, breakpoints and watchpoints are some of the most powerful features that help developers track down and fix issues in their code. In this section, we'll explore advanced breakpoint and watchpoint techniques to aid in debugging iOS applications.

Breakpoint Actions

Conditional Breakpoints

Conditional breakpoints allow you to pause execution only when a specific condition is met. To set a conditional breakpoint:

1. Right-click on an existing breakpoint and select "Edit Breakpoint."
2. In the breakpoint settings, enter a condition. For example, you can specify a variable value to break when it reaches a certain threshold.

Conditional breakpoints are handy when you want to investigate a problem under specific circumstances without stopping execution every time.

Log Messages

Breakpoints can be enhanced with log messages, which print information to the Xcode console when the breakpoint is hit. To add a log message to a breakpoint:

1. Right-click on a breakpoint and select "Edit Breakpoint."
2. In the breakpoint settings, add an action to "Log Message." Enter the message you want to log.

This is useful for tracking the values of variables or objects at a specific point in your code.

Debugging Actions

You can also execute code when a breakpoint is hit by adding a "Debugger Command" action. This is particularly helpful when you need to make on-the-fly changes during debugging without modifying your source code. To add a debugger command:

1. Right-click on a breakpoint and select "Edit Breakpoint."
2. In the breakpoint settings, add an action to "Debugger Command." Enter the Swift code you want to execute.

Debugger commands can help you tweak variables or perform specific actions to investigate issues more effectively.

Exception Breakpoints

Exception breakpoints are another valuable tool for debugging iOS apps. They pause execution when an exception is thrown, allowing you to catch and diagnose errors as soon as they occur. To set an exception breakpoint:

1. Open the breakpoint navigator in Xcode.
2. Click the "+" button at the bottom left and choose "Exception Breakpoint."
3. You can configure it to break on all exceptions or specific types of exceptions.

Exception breakpoints help you identify and resolve errors like unhandled exceptions, making your app more robust.

Watchpoints

Watchpoints are specialized breakpoints that trigger when a variable's value changes. This is extremely useful for tracking down bugs related to the modification of specific variables. To set a watchpoint:

1. Right-click on an existing breakpoint and select "Edit Breakpoint."
2. In the breakpoint settings, add an action to "Watch Variable." Enter the variable name you want to monitor.

Watchpoints are invaluable for identifying when and where a variable's value is modified unexpectedly, aiding in debugging complex code.

Conclusion

Advanced breakpoint and watchpoint techniques in Xcode empower iOS developers to diagnose and fix issues efficiently. By using conditional breakpoints, log messages, debugger commands, exception breakpoints, and watchpoints, you can gain deeper insights into your code's behavior and quickly resolve problems, ultimately leading to more stable and reliable iOS applications.

Section 13.3: Debugging Multithreaded Applications

Debugging multithreaded applications can be a challenging task, especially when dealing with concurrent code that runs on multiple threads simultaneously. In this section, we'll explore techniques and tools for debugging multithreaded iOS applications using Xcode.

Thread Sanitizer

Xcode offers a powerful tool called the Thread Sanitizer (TSan), which helps detect data races and other multithreading issues in your code. To enable Thread Sanitizer:

1. Open your Xcode project.
2. Navigate to the "Product" menu.
3. Choose "Scheme" and then "Edit Scheme."
4. In the scheme settings, select the "Run" phase.
5. Under the "Diagnostics" tab, check the "Thread Sanitizer" option.

Once enabled, build and run your application, and the Thread Sanitizer will report any multithreading issues it detects. This includes data races, deadlocks, and other concurrency problems. TSan provides valuable insights into where and why these issues occur, helping you identify and fix them.

Breakpoints and Thread Focus

Xcode allows you to set breakpoints that are specific to particular threads, which can be useful for isolating and debugging multithreading issues. To set breakpoints for specific threads:

1. Add a breakpoint at the location in your code where you suspect a problem.
2. Right-click the breakpoint and choose "Edit Breakpoint."
3. Under the "Thread" section, select "Automatically continue after evaluating actions."

With this configuration, the breakpoint will only stop the thread that hits it while allowing other threads to continue executing. This is beneficial when you want to investigate issues occurring on specific threads without disrupting the entire application.

Debugging Concurrency with DispatchQueue

Swift's DispatchQueue is a fundamental component of multithreaded programming on iOS. While debugging concurrency issues, you can use DispatchQueue to your advantage. For instance, you can:

- Use DispatchQueue.main.async to update the UI from a background thread to ensure UI updates occur on the main thread.

- Create serial queues to ensure certain tasks run sequentially to avoid data race conditions.

- Utilize concurrent queues for parallelizing tasks that don't have data dependencies.

By understanding and using DispatchQueue effectively, you can prevent and debug concurrency issues more efficiently.

Analyzing Thread States

Xcode provides a Threads Debug Navigator that allows you to inspect the state of each thread in your application. To access it:

1. Open Xcode and run your application.
2. Go to the "View" menu and choose "Debug Area" > "Show Debug Area."
3. In the Debug Area, select the "Debug Navigator" tab.
4. You'll see a list of threads along with their current state and stack traces.

The Threads Debug Navigator provides insights into which threads are active, paused, or xtopped. You can inspect thread call stacks to identify potential issues, such as threads waiting for a resource or threads that are stuck in a particular function.

Conclusion

Debugging multithreaded iOS applications can be complex due to the concurrent nature of threaded code. However, by leveraging tools like Thread Sanitizer, setting breakpoints for specific threads, understanding DispatchQueue, and analyzing thread states in Xcode, you can effectively identify and resolve multithreading issues, ensuring the stability and reliability of your iOS app.

Section 13.4: Profiling with Instruments

Instruments is a powerful profiling and performance analysis tool that comes bundled with Xcode. It enables you to monitor various aspects of your iOS app's performance, including CPU usage, memory usage, and more. Profiling your app with Instruments can help you identify bottlenecks, memory leaks, and performance issues, allowing you to optimize your app for a better user experience.

Launching Instruments

To start profiling your app with Instruments, follow these steps:

1. Open Xcode and your project.
2. Go to the "Product" menu and choose "Profile."
3. Select the profiling template that matches your use case. For example, you can choose the "Time Profiler" template to analyze CPU usage or the "Leaks" template to detect memory leaks.
4. Click the "Profile" button, and Instruments will launch with your app.

Profiling CPU Usage

The "Time Profiler" instrument in Instruments allows you to analyze CPU usage over time. It shows you a detailed view of which functions and methods are consuming CPU resources and how much time is spent in each.

To use the "Time Profiler" instrument:

1. In Instruments, select the "Time Profiler" template.
2. Click the red "Record" button to start profiling.
3. Interact with your app as you normally would.
4. Click the "Stop" button to end the profiling session.

In the results, you'll see a list of functions and methods sorted by CPU usage, making it easy to identify performance bottlenecks in your code. You can click on specific functions to see their call stack and pinpoint the source of the performance issue.

Detecting Memory Leaks

Memory leaks can lead to increased memory usage and degraded app performance. The "Leaks" instrument in Instruments helps you identify and fix memory leaks in your app.

To detect memory leaks:

1. In Instruments, select the "Leaks" template.
2. Click the red "Record" button and use your app.
3. After some time, click the "Stop" button.

Instruments will display any memory leaks it detects, including information about the leaked objects and where they were allocated in your code. This information is invaluable for tracking down and resolving memory-related issues.

Analyzing Energy Usage

Battery life is crucial for mobile devices, so understanding your app's energy usage is essential. The "Energy Impact" instrument in Instruments provides insights into how your app affects the device's energy consumption.

To analyze energy usage:

1. In Instruments, select the "Energy Impact" template.
2. Click the red "Record" button and interact with your app.
3. Stop the recording when you're done.

You'll see an energy impact graph that shows your app's power usage over time. This can help you identify parts of your app that consume excessive energy and make necessary optimizations.

Conclusion

Profiling with Instruments is a vital step in optimizing your iOS app's performance and ensuring it runs smoothly. Whether you're concerned about CPU usage, memory leaks, or energy efficiency, Instruments provides the tools and insights you need to diagnose and resolve issues. Regular profiling and performance analysis should be part of your development workflow to deliver high-quality apps to your users.

Section 13.5: Static Analysis and Code Coverage

Static analysis and code coverage are essential practices in software development that help ensure the quality, reliability, and security of your iOS applications. In this section, we will explore the concepts and tools related to static code analysis and code coverage for iOS development.

Static Analysis

Static analysis is the process of examining your source code without executing it. It aims to identify potential issues, such as code smells, bugs, and security vulnerabilities, by analyzing the code's structure, syntax, and semantics. Static analysis tools can provide valuable insights into your codebase and help you maintain code quality.

Using Static Analysis Tools

Xcode comes with built-in static analysis tools that can help you detect common issues in your code. To use these tools, follow these steps:

1. Open your Xcode project.
2. Select the target you want to analyze.
3. Go to the "Product" menu and choose "Analyze."

Xcode will perform static analysis on your code and report any issues it finds. You can click on each issue to see more details and navigate to the problematic code. It's essential to regularly run static analysis to catch potential problems early in the development process.

Code Coverage

Code coverage is a metric that measures the percentage of your code that is executed during testing. It helps you understand how thoroughly your tests exercise your codebase. Higher code coverage indicates better test coverage, but it doesn't guarantee the absence of bugs.

Using Code Coverage Tools

Xcode provides code coverage tools that can help you assess your test suite's effectiveness. To use code coverage in Xcode:

1. Open your Xcode project.
2. Select the scheme for your unit tests.
3. Go to the "Product" menu and choose "Perform Action" and then "Test Without Building."

Xcode will execute your unit tests and display the code coverage results in the editor area. You'll see color-coded overlays on your source code files, indicating which lines were executed during testing. Green lines were executed, while red lines were not.

Benefits of Static Analysis and Code Coverage

Static analysis and code coverage offer several benefits:

1. **Early Issue Detection**: Static analysis helps catch potential issues before runtime, reducing the chances of bugs and vulnerabilities reaching your users.
2. **Improved Code Quality**: By identifying code smells and enforcing coding standards, static analysis tools promote better coding practices.
3. **Test Effectiveness**: Code coverage helps you assess the comprehensiveness of your test suite and identify areas that require additional testing.
4. **Security**: Static analysis can uncover security vulnerabilities, such as code injection or data leaks, before they become exploitable.
5. **Maintainability**: Regular use of these tools can make your codebase more maintainable and easier to work with over

time.

Incorporating static analysis and code coverage into your development workflow can lead to more reliable and secure iOS applications.

Conclusion

Static analysis and code coverage are crucial tools in the iOS developer's toolkit. They help you maintain code quality, detect issues early, and assess the effectiveness of your tests. By integrating these practices into your development process, you can ensure that your iOS apps are more robust, reliable, and secure. Regularly reviewing and improving your code using these tools will contribute to the long-term success of your projects.

Chapter 14: Enhancing App Performance

Section 14.1: Performance Optimization Techniques

In the world of iOS app development, performance is a critical aspect that can significantly impact user satisfaction and app success. Users expect apps to be fast, responsive, and efficient. Slow and sluggish apps can lead to user frustration and negative reviews. In this section, we will explore various performance optimization techniques that can help you improve the speed and efficiency of your iOS applications.

1. Profiling Your App

Before you can optimize your app's performance, it's essential to identify bottlenecks and areas that need improvement. Profiling tools like Instruments in Xcode can provide valuable insights into your app's behavior. Use Instruments to monitor CPU usage, memory usage, and network activity. By profiling your app, you can pinpoint performance issues and focus your optimization efforts.

2. Memory Management

Efficient memory management is crucial for app performance. Memory leaks, where your app holds onto memory that is no longer needed, can lead to slowdowns and crashes. Use Xcode's memory debugging tools to identify and fix memory leaks. Additionally, consider using Swift's Automatic Reference Counting (ARC) to manage memory automatically.

3. Optimizing User Interface (UI)

The user interface is one of the most visible parts of your app, and optimizing it is essential for a smooth user experience. Use techniques like lazy loading for UI elements, reuse cells in table views and collection views, and minimize the use of complex animations that can slow down your app's responsiveness.

4. Background Processing

Perform resource-intensive tasks in the background to keep your app responsive. Use Grand Central Dispatch (GCD) or Operation Queues to offload tasks like data processing and image loading. This prevents the main thread from becoming blocked and ensures that the UI remains responsive.

5. Reducing Network Usage

Network requests can introduce latency and affect your app's performance. Minimize the number of network requests by using techniques like batch processing and caching. Implement pagination for large data sets to load only the data needed for the current screen.

6. Optimizing Algorithms and Data Structures

Review your app's algorithms and data structures to ensure they are efficient. Use appropriate data structures for tasks like searching and sorting. Consider algorithmic optimizations to reduce computation time and memory usage.

7. Code Profiling

Use code profiling tools to identify sections of your code that are consuming significant CPU time. Profile your code to detect hotspots and bottlenecks. Once identified, focus on optimizing these sections for better performance.

8. Efficient Resource Management

Optimize the management of resources such as images, videos, and audio files. Use appropriate compression techniques to reduce the size of these resources without compromising quality. Load resources lazily when needed to conserve memory.

9. Testing and Benchmarking

Regularly test your app's performance on various iOS devices and versions. Benchmark your app's performance against predefined criteria to ensure it meets performance goals. Automated testing and continuous integration can help catch performance regressions early.

10. App Thinning and Optimization Strategies

Leverage app thinning techniques provided by Apple to reduce the size of your app for downloads and updates. These techniques include slicing, on-demand resources, and bitcode. Smaller app sizes can lead to faster downloads and better user experiences.

Optimizing the performance of your iOS app is an ongoing process that requires continuous monitoring and improvement. By following these techniques and leveraging the tools provided by Xcode and Apple, you can create iOS applications that are not only feature-rich but also deliver a fast and responsive user experience. Remember that performance optimization is a balance between features and speed, so prioritize optimizations based on user expectations and app requirements.

Section 14.2: Efficient Memory Usage

Efficient memory usage is a critical aspect of app performance. When your iOS app uses memory efficiently, it not only runs faster but also provides a smoother user experience. In this section, we'll explore various strategies and best practices for managing memory effectively in your iOS applications.

1. Automatic Reference Counting (ARC)

ARC is a memory management technique in Swift that automatically manages the allocation and deallocation of memory for objects. With ARC, you don't need to manually release memory, as it is done for you when objects are no longer needed. By default, new projects in Xcode use ARC, but if you're working with legacy code or C/C++ libraries, you may need to manage memory manually using retain and release.

2. Use Structs When Appropriate

In Swift, structs are value types and are stored directly in memory where they are declared. Unlike classes, which are reference types, structs are copied when passed around in your code. Use structs for simple data types like coordinates, sizes, and colors. This can reduce memory overhead, especially when dealing with large arrays or collections of these types.

```
struct Point {

var x: Double

var y: Double

}

var myPoint = Point(x: 10.0, y: 20.0)
```

3. Managing Caches

Caching frequently used data, such as images or network responses, can improve app performance and reduce unnecessary memory usage. Implement a caching mechanism that stores data in memory temporarily and clears it when memory pressure increases. You can use libraries like NSCache to manage in-memory caches efficiently.

```swift
let cache = NSCache<NSString, UIImage>()

// Store an image in the cache

cache.setObject(image, forKey: "imageKey")

// Retrieve an image from the cache

if let cachedImage = cache.object(forKey: "imageKey") {

// Use the cached image

}
```

4. Lazy Loading

Lazy loading is a technique where you load resources or initialize objects only when they are needed. For example, you can delay the loading of images until they are about to be displayed on the screen. This reduces the initial memory footprint of your app and improves the app's launch time.

```swift
class MyViewController: UIViewController {

@IBOutlet weak var imageView: UIImageView!

lazy var image: UIImage = {

// Load the image when it's accessed for the first time
```

```
return UIImage(named: "myImage")!

}()

override func viewDidLoad() {

super.viewDidLoad()

// The image is loaded only when accessed

imageView.image = image

}

}
```

5. Deallocating Unused Objects

Ensure that objects are deallocated when they are no longer needed. This is particularly important for view controllers and large objects. Implement the deinit method to release resources and perform cleanup when an object is deallocated.

```
class MyViewController: UIViewController {

// ...

deinit {

// Perform cleanup when the view controller is deallocated

}

}
```

6. Avoid Strong Reference Cycles

Strong reference cycles, also known as retain cycles, occur when two or more objects hold strong references to each other, preventing them from being deallocated. To avoid retain cycles, use weak or unowned references when appropriate, especially in closures and delegate relationships.

```swift
class MyClass {

var completionHandler: (() -> Void)?

func performAsyncTask() {

// Avoid a strong reference cycle by using [weak self]

DispatchQueue.global().async { [weak self] in

// Check if self still exists

guard let self = self else { return }

// Perform the task

self.completionHandler?()

}

}

}
```

7. Monitoring Memory Usage

Use Xcode's built-in tools, such as the Memory Graph Debugger and Instruments, to monitor memory usage and identify memory leaks and retain cycles. These tools provide visual representations of your app's memory usage and help you pinpoint issues for resolution.

Efficient memory usage is a fundamental aspect of iOS app development that directly impacts user experience. By following these memory management best practices and regularly profiling your app's memory usage, you can create apps that are both performant and reliable. Remember that memory management is an ongoing process, and it's essential to test your app on different devices and scenarios to ensure optimal memory performance.

Section 14.3: Optimizing CPU and Battery Usage

Optimizing CPU and battery usage is crucial for delivering a smooth and power-efficient user experience in your iOS applications. In this section, we'll explore various strategies and best practices for optimizing CPU and battery usage in your iOS apps.

1. Use Background Tasks Wisely

Background tasks are essential for apps that need to perform work when not in the foreground. However, excessive use of background tasks can drain the device's battery quickly. Ensure that you only use background tasks when necessary and follow the guidelines set by Apple for background execution.

```
// Register for background task

let                backgroundTaskID                =
UIApplication.shared.beginBackgroundTask(withName:
"MyBackgroundTask") {

// Clean up and end the task

UIApplication.shared.endBackgroundTask(backgroundTaskID)

}
```

```
// Perform background work

// ...

// End the background task when done

UIApplication.shared.endBackgroundTask(backgroundTaskID)
```

2. Threading and Concurrency

Efficiently managing threads and concurrency can significantly impact CPU and battery usage. Use GCD (Grand Central Dispatch) and Operation Queues to perform tasks concurrently and avoid blocking the main thread. This keeps the UI responsive and reduces CPU load.

```
let queue = DispatchQueue.global(qos: .background)

queue.async {

// Perform work on a background queue

// ...

DispatchQueue.main.async {

// Update the UI on the main thread

// ...

}

}
```

3. Energy Profiling with Instruments

Xcode's Instruments tool provides an Energy Impact profiler, allowing you to measure the energy consumption of your app. Use this profiler to identify areas of your app that consume excessive CPU and energy. Addressing these issues can lead to significant battery life improvements.

4. Idle Timers and Background Modes

iOS offers background modes for certain types of apps, such as navigation or audio apps, to keep running even when in the background. If your app doesn't require continuous background operation, disable these modes to conserve battery life. Additionally, avoid using unnecessary timers and ensure they are properly invalidated when no longer needed.

// Disable idle timer (prevent screen from sleeping)

UIApplication.shared.isIdleTimerDisabled = **true**

5. Network Efficiency

Efficiently managing network requests can reduce both CPU and battery usage. Use Apple's URLSession for networking and ensure that you follow best practices, such as batching requests, using background transfers, and handling errors gracefully.

6. Core Location and GPS

Location-based apps that continuously use GPS can consume significant battery power. Minimize GPS usage when your app is in the background or use region monitoring to reduce the need for constant location updates.

7. Optimize Animations

Smooth animations enhance the user experience but can be resource-intensive. Optimize animations by reducing their complexity and using the Core Animation framework efficiently. Avoid excessive use of UIView animations, as they can consume CPU resources.

8. Background Audio and Media Playback

If your app plays audio or video in the background, ensure efficient media playback to minimize CPU usage. Use background audio modes and implement audio buffering to prevent playback interruptions.

try? AVAudioSession.sharedInstance().setCategory(.playback, mode: **.default**, options: [])

try? AVAudioSession.sharedInstance().setActive(**true**)

9. Power Monitoring

Use the UIDevice class to monitor battery state and level. You can adjust your app's behavior based on whether the device is plugged in or running on battery. This allows you to conserve power when needed.

let batteryLevel = UIDevice.current.batteryLevel

let batteryState = UIDevice.current.batteryState

if batteryState == .unplugged && batteryLevel < 0.2 {

// *Implement power-saving measures*

}

10. Regularly Test on Low-End Devices

To ensure that your app performs well on a wide range of devices, regularly test it on low-end or older iOS devices. These devices often have less powerful CPUs and smaller batteries, making them good indicators of potential performance and battery life issues.

By following these best practices for optimizing CPU and battery usage, you can create iOS apps that are not only responsive and performant but also kind to your users' device batteries. Remember that a well-optimized app not only improves the user experience but also helps retain users and receive positive reviews on the App Store.

Section 14.4: Network Performance Tuning

Network performance is a critical aspect of modern mobile app development. Users expect apps to be responsive and efficient when interacting with remote services and fetching data. In this section, we'll explore various strategies and best practices for tuning the network performance of your iOS applications.

1. Use Efficient Data Formats

When designing your app's API, choose efficient data formats like JSON over XML, as they are typically more compact and easier to parse. Minimize unnecessary data in responses to reduce the amount of data transmitted over the network. You can also implement compression techniques like gzip or Brotli to further reduce payload size.

```swift
// Example using URLSession to fetch JSON data

let url = URL(string: "https://api.example.com/data.json")!

let task = URLSession.shared.dataTask(with: url) { data, _, error in

if let error = error {

print("Error: \(error)")
```

```swift
return
}

if let data = data {

do {

let json = try JSONSerialization.jsonObject(with: data, options: [])

// Process JSON data

} catch {

print("JSON parsing error: \(error)")

}

}

}

task.resume()
```

2. Pagination and Lazy Loading

Instead of loading large datasets at once, implement pagination or lazy loading to fetch data incrementally as needed. This reduces the initial load time and conserves bandwidth. Use query parameters to specify the number of items per page and the page number.

```swift
// Example API request for pagination

let page = 1

let itemsPerPage = 20

let apiUrl = "https://api.example.com/data?page=\(page)&per_page=\(itemsPerPage)"
```

3. Caching

Implement caching mechanisms to store frequently accessed data locally. This reduces the need to fetch the same data repeatedly from the server. Use the URLCache class provided by URLSession for simple in-memory caching.

```swift
let cache = URLCache.shared

let config = URLSessionConfiguration.default

config.urlCache = cache

let session = URLSession(configuration: config)
```

4. Background Fetching

Leverage background fetching to update data periodically, even when your app is not in the foreground. Use the Background Fetch capability provided by iOS to fetch fresh data and update the cache. This ensures that the user always has access to the latest information.

```swift
// Example background fetch implementation

func application(_ application: UIApplication, performFetchWithCompletionHandler completionHandler: @escaping (UIBackgroundFetchResult) -> Void) {

// Perform background data fetch here

// Update cache and notify the completion handler

completionHandler(.newData)

}
```

5. Optimize Images

Images often contribute significantly to the size of network responses. Optimize images by using appropriate image formats (e.g., WebP or JPEG) and resolutions. Implement lazy loading for images that are not immediately visible on the screen to avoid unnecessary downloads.

6. Reduce Network Requests

Minimize the number of network requests your app makes. Combine multiple requests into a single request when possible (batching). Additionally, consider using WebSocket for real-time updates instead of polling the server frequently.

// Example WebSocket implementation using Starscream library

```swift
import Starscream

let socket = WebSocket(url: URL(string: "wss://api.example.com/socket")!)

socket.onConnect = {

print("WebSocket connected")

}

socket.onDisconnect = { error in

print("WebSocket disconnected: \(error?.localizedDescription ?? "Unknown error")")

}

socket.onText = { text in
```

```swift
print("Received text from WebSocket: \(text)")
```

```swift
}
```

```swift
socket.connect()
```

7. Monitor and Handle Connectivity Changes

Detect changes in network connectivity and respond accordingly. Use the NetworkReachability API to monitor network status and provide appropriate feedback to the user when the connection is lost.

```swift
// Example network reachability monitoring

let reachability = try? Reachability()

reachability?.whenReachable = { _ in

// Network is reachable

}

reachability?.whenUnreachable = { _ in

// Network is unreachable

}

try? reachability?.startNotifier()
```

8. Error Handling and Retries

Implement robust error handling and retries for network requests. Handle common errors such as timeouts, connection failures, and server errors gracefully. Implement retry mechanisms with exponential backoff to avoid overwhelming the server with retry attempts.

```swift
// Example retry mechanism

func retryRequest(request: URLRequest, maxRetries: Int,
completion: @escaping (Data?, URLResponse?, Error?) -> Void) {

var retries = 0

func performRequest() {

let task = URLSession.shared.dataTask(with: request) { data,
response, error in

if let error = error, retries < maxRetries {

retries += 1

DispatchQueue.global().asyncAfter(deadline: .now() + pow(2,
Double(retries))) {

performRequest()

}

} else {

completion(data, response, error)

}

}

task.resume()

}

performRequest()

}
```

9. Optimize for Cellular Data Usage

Many users have limited cellular data plans. Consider providing options in your app settings to allow users to control when and how much data is consumed. Implement features like "Wi-Fi-only downloads" and "data-saving mode" to cater to these users' needs.

By implementing these network performance tuning techniques, you can create iOS apps that provide a fast and efficient user experience while conserving the user's data plan and battery life. Ensuring your app performs well under varying network conditions is essential for user satisfaction and retention.

Section 14.5: App Thinning and Optimization Strategies

App thinning is a set of techniques provided by Apple to reduce the size of your app and optimize its performance. These strategies ensure that your app consumes fewer system resources, loads faster, and takes up less storage space on the user's device. In this section, we'll explore various app thinning and optimization techniques to improve the overall user experience.

1. Asset Catalogs and On-Demand Resources

Use asset catalogs to organize your app's images and other media files. Asset catalogs allow you to create image sets for different device resolutions and screen sizes. Additionally, you can take advantage of on-demand resources to load assets dynamically as needed, reducing the initial app size.

```
// Loading an on-demand resource

let assetTag = "highResImage"
```

```swift
let resourceRequest = NSBundleResourceRequest(tags: [assetTag])

resourceRequest.beginAccessingResources { error in

if let error = error {

print("Error loading on-demand resource: \(error)")

} else {

// Use the loaded resource

}

}
```

2. Bitcode

Enable Bitcode when building your app. Bitcode is an intermediate representation of your app's compiled code that allows Apple to re-optimize your app for different devices and architectures. This can lead to smaller app sizes and better performance on specific devices.

3. App Slicing

App slicing is a technique that ensures users download only the necessary app assets for their device. When users install your app, the App Store serves them a version of your app optimized for their specific device, reducing unnecessary assets and saving storage space.

4. Thinning and Bitcode Compatibility

Ensure that any third-party libraries or frameworks you use are compatible with app thinning and Bitcode. Some libraries may not support these features, which can result in larger app sizes.

5. Reduce Unnecessary Code and Resources

Regularly review your codebase and remove any unused or obsolete code and resources. This not only reduces the app's size but also makes maintenance easier. Tools like Xcode's "Unused Resources" feature can help identify and remove unused assets.

6. Symbol Stripping

Enable "Dead Code Stripping" in your Xcode project settings. This feature removes unused functions and classes from your app's binary during the build process, resulting in a smaller executable size.

7. Optimize Launch Time

Optimize your app's launch time by deferring non-essential tasks to a later time. Lazy-load resources and perform initializations as needed, rather than during app launch. This ensures that the app becomes responsive to user input more quickly.

8. Universal Links and Deep Linking

Implement Universal Links and deep linking to navigate users to specific parts of your app directly from web links or other apps. This reduces the need to bundle all possible screens and assets into the main app binary, further reducing its size.

9. Regular Updates and Maintenance

Regularly update your app and its dependencies to take advantage of the latest optimization techniques and improvements. Apple frequently releases updates and tools to help developers optimize their apps for performance and size.

10. Testing on Real Devices

Test your app on real devices to ensure that app thinning works as expected. Sometimes, issues may arise when certain assets or resources are not downloaded correctly on specific devices.

By incorporating these app thinning and optimization strategies into your iOS app development workflow, you can create apps that not only perform better but also provide a more efficient and enjoyable experience for your users. Reducing app size and optimizing performance are key factors in attracting and retaining users in today's competitive app market.

Chapter 15: UI/UX Design Principles

Section 15.1: Principles of Good UI/UX Design

Good user interface (UI) and user experience (UX) design is fundamental to the success of any app. It can be the difference between an app that users love and one they quickly abandon. In this section, we'll explore the principles of good UI/UX design and how they can be applied to create engaging and user-friendly iOS applications.

1. User-Centered Design

User-centered design is the foundation of good UI/UX. It involves understanding your target audience, their needs, and their pain points. Conduct user research, gather feedback, and create personas to represent your typical users. Design your app with their preferences and behaviors in mind.

2. Consistency

Consistency in design elements, such as buttons, fonts, colors, and navigation, is crucial for a seamless user experience. Maintain a consistent visual style and layout throughout your app to make it feel cohesive and intuitive.

```swift
// Swift code for consistent button styling

let button = UIButton()

button.setTitle("Submit", for: .normal)

button.backgroundColor = .blue
```

```
button.setTitleColor(.white, for: .normal)
```

```
button.layer.cornerRadius = 8
```

3. Simplicity

Simplicity is the key to an intuitive UI. Avoid clutter and complexity by simplifying user interfaces. Remove unnecessary elements and features that can overwhelm users. Present information and options in a clear and straightforward manner.

4. Navigation and Hierarchy

Create a logical and hierarchical navigation flow within your app. Users should easily understand where they are in the app and how to navigate to other sections. Use clear labels, breadcrumbs, and intuitive icons for navigation.

5. Feedback and Affordance

Provide feedback to users when they perform actions. Use animations, tooltips, or status messages to confirm that an action was successful. Buttons and interactive elements should have visual affordance, making it clear that they are clickable or tappable.

```
// Swift code for providing feedback with animations
```

```
UIView.animate(withDuration: 0.3) {
```

```
// Apply a highlight or animation to indicate an action
```

```
button.backgroundColor = .green
```

```
}
```

6. Accessibility

Consider accessibility from the start of your design process. Ensure that your app is usable by people with disabilities, including those with visual or hearing impairments. Use semantic HTML elements and provide alternative text for images.

7. Aesthetics

A visually appealing design can enhance the user experience. Pay attention to color schemes, typography, and spacing. Use white space effectively to reduce visual clutter and improve readability.

8. User Testing

Regularly conduct usability testing with real users to gather feedback and identify pain points. Use usability testing tools to record user interactions and analyze their behavior within the app. Iteratively refine your design based on user feedback.

9. Responsive Design

Design your app to be responsive to different screen sizes and orientations. Ensure that your UI elements adapt gracefully to various devices, from iPhones to iPads.

10. Prototyping

Create interactive prototypes to test your app's design before development. Prototyping tools allow you to simulate user interactions and validate your design decisions without writing code.

11. Continuous Improvement

UI/UX design is an ongoing process. Continuously gather user feedback, monitor app analytics, and make iterative improvements to enhance the user experience. Keep up with design trends and adapt your app accordingly.

By adhering to these principles of good UI/UX design, you can create iOS applications that not only look visually appealing but also provide a user-friendly and enjoyable experience. Remember that a well-designed app can lead to higher user satisfaction, better retention rates, and increased success in the competitive app market.

Section 15.2: Designing for Different Devices

Designing for different iOS devices, such as iPhones and iPads, is a crucial aspect of UI/UX design. Each device has its unique screen size, aspect ratio, and capabilities, and your app should adapt gracefully to provide an optimal user experience on all of them.

1. Understanding Device Variability

iOS devices come in various sizes and resolutions. iPhones range from the compact iPhone SE to the larger iPhone Pro Max, while iPads have different screen sizes, from the iPad Mini to the iPad Pro. Understanding this variability is essential for designing responsive interfaces.

2. Adaptive Layouts

To accommodate different screen sizes, use adaptive layouts. Apple's Auto Layout system allows you to create flexible and responsive UIs that adjust based on available screen space. Define constraints between UI elements to maintain their relative positions.

```swift
// Swift code for Auto Layout constraints

let titleLabel = UILabel()

titleLabel.translatesAutoresizingMaskIntoConstraints = false

view.addSubview(titleLabel)

// Center the label horizontally

titleLabel.centerXAnchor.constraint(equalTo:
view.centerXAnchor).isActive = true

// Position the label 20 points from the top

titleLabel.topAnchor.constraint(equalTo:        view.topAnchor,
constant: 20).isActive = true
```

3. Universal Design

Whenever possible, design your app to be universal. This means creating a single app that works well on both iPhones and iPads. Universal apps can reach a broader audience and simplify development and maintenance.

4. Size Classes

Size classes in Interface Builder allow you to customize your UI for different screen sizes. You can create variations of your layout for regular and compact width or height environments. For example, you might adjust the layout for landscape and portrait orientations.

5. Adaptive Fonts and Typography

Use dynamic type and adaptive fonts to ensure that text remains readable across various devices and accessibility settings. Allow users to adjust the font size within your app by respecting the Dynamic Type settings in iOS.

// Swift code for using dynamic type

titleLabel.font = UIFont.preferredFont(forTextStyle: .headline)

6. Device-Specific Features

Take advantage of device-specific features. For example, iPads support multitasking with Split View and Slide Over, allowing users to interact with multiple apps simultaneously. Consider how your app can leverage these features to enhance the user experience.

7. iPad-Specific Design

If you're designing specifically for iPad, utilize the larger screen real estate to provide more content or additional features. Create interfaces that make use of the iPad's multitasking capabilities, such as displaying multiple panels or sidebars.

8. Responsive Images

Optimize images for different screen resolutions and sizes. Use vector graphics and scalable assets to ensure that images remain sharp and clear on all devices. Consider using asset catalogs to manage image assets for various resolutions.

9. Testing on Real Devices

Always test your app on real devices to verify that your designs adapt as expected. Different devices may have different performance characteristics, and testing helps ensure smooth interactions and responsiveness.

10. User Feedback

Listen to user feedback, especially from users with different devices. They can provide valuable insights into any issues or improvements needed for specific devices.

Designing for different iOS devices requires careful planning and consideration. By creating responsive and adaptive layouts, using device-specific features, and conducting thorough testing, you can ensure that your app provides a consistent and enjoyable user experience across the entire iOS ecosystem.

Section 15.3: User Testing and Feedback

User testing and feedback are integral parts of the UI/UX design process. They help you understand how real users interact with your app, identify pain points, and make informed design decisions to improve the user experience. In this section, we'll explore the importance of user testing and feedback and the best practices to implement them effectively.

1. The Importance of User Testing

User testing involves observing real users as they interact with your app. This process provides valuable insights into how users perceive and use your app, highlighting areas that require improvement. Here's why user testing is crucial:

- **Identifying Usability Issues:** User testing uncovers usability issues, such as confusing navigation, unintuitive interfaces, or unclear instructions.

- **Validating Design Decisions:** It validates whether your design decisions align with users' expectations and needs.

- **Enhancing User Satisfaction:** By addressing user pain points, you can improve overall user satisfaction and retention.

- **Optimizing Conversion Rates:** For e-commerce or conversion-focused apps, user testing can help optimize the user journey and increase conversion rates.

2. Setting Clear Objectives

Before conducting user testing, define clear objectives. What do you want to learn or validate through testing? Common objectives include understanding user workflows, evaluating specific features, or assessing the overall user experience.

3. Recruiting Participants

Recruit a diverse group of participants who represent your target audience. Depending on your app's demographics, consider factors like age, gender, location, and tech-savviness. Aim for a mix of both experienced and novice users.

4. Creating Test Scenarios

Design realistic test scenarios that reflect how users would naturally interact with your app. Provide participants with tasks or scenarios to complete while using the app. For example, "Find and purchase a product" for an e-commerce app.

5. Observing and Gathering Data

During user testing, observe participants as they navigate through your app. Pay attention to their interactions, comments, and pain points. You can record sessions for later analysis.

6. Collecting Feedback

After each testing session, collect qualitative feedback from participants. Ask open-ended questions about their experience, likes, dislikes, and suggestions for improvement.

7. Iterative Design

Use the insights gained from user testing to iterate on your app's design. Address usability issues, refine features, and make improvements. The iterative design process ensures your app evolves based on user feedback.

8. Remote and In-Person Testing

User testing can be conducted remotely or in person. Remote testing offers flexibility and allows you to reach a broader audience, while in-person testing provides immediate feedback and deeper insights.

9. Usability Testing Tools

Consider using usability testing tools and platforms that facilitate user testing and data collection. Some tools even provide heatmaps and user session recordings for more in-depth analysis.

10. Continuous Feedback Loop

User testing should be an ongoing process throughout your app's development lifecycle. Regularly gather feedback and make improvements to ensure a user-centric design.

11. A/B Testing

A/B testing involves presenting different variations of your app to users to determine which performs better. It's an effective way to optimize specific features or UI elements based on real user preferences.

12. Accessibility Testing

Include users with disabilities in your testing to ensure your app is accessible to everyone. Test with screen readers, keyboard navigation, and other assistive technologies.

13. Privacy and Consent

Respect user privacy and obtain their informed consent before recording or collecting any data during user testing. Explain how their data will be used and stored.

User testing and feedback are vital steps in creating a user-centered app. By involving real users, setting clear objectives, and continuously iterating on your design, you can create an app that meets users' needs, delights them, and achieves your business goals.

Section 15.4: Color Theory and Typography in Apps

Color theory and typography are fundamental aspects of UI/UX design that significantly impact the visual appeal and usability of your app. In this section, we'll explore the importance of color and typography choices, best practices, and how they contribute to creating a cohesive and effective user interface.

1. The Role of Color in UI/UX Design

Color plays a crucial role in conveying information, setting the mood, and establishing brand identity within your app. Here's how you can leverage color effectively:

- **Consistency:** Define a color palette and stick to it throughout your app. Consistency in color usage enhances recognition and usability.

- **Hierarchy:** Use color to establish hierarchy within your app's interface. For example, important actions or elements can be highlighted using a distinct color.

- **Accessibility:** Ensure your color choices meet accessibility standards. Consider users with visual impairments and use sufficient contrast between text and background colors.

- **Branding:** Your app's color scheme should align with your brand identity. Consistency in branding builds trust and recognition among users.

2. Choosing a Color Palette

When selecting a color palette, consider factors like your app's target audience, its purpose, and the emotions you want to evoke. Here are some considerations:

- **Primary and Secondary Colors:** Define primary and secondary colors to maintain consistency and balance.

- **Complementary Colors:** Use color theory principles to select complementary colors that work well together and create visually appealing combinations.

- **Color Psychology:** Different colors evoke specific emotions. Research color psychology to align your color choices with the desired user experience.

3. Typography Choices

Typography is another critical aspect of UI/UX design that affects readability, user engagement, and the overall aesthetics of your app. Here are some typography considerations:

- **Font Selection:** Choose fonts that are legible and align with your app's style. Consider using a combination of fonts for headings and body text.

- **Hierarchy:** Establish a typographic hierarchy with varying font sizes, styles, and weights to guide users' attention and improve readability.

- **Spacing and Line Height:** Adequate spacing between lines and characters enhances readability, especially on small screens.

- **Responsiveness:** Ensure that your chosen fonts and typography settings are responsive and adapt well to different screen sizes and orientations.

4. Testing and Feedback

Testing your color and typography choices with real users is essential. Conduct user testing to gather feedback on how users perceive and interact with your app's visual elements.

5. Prototyping Tools

Utilize prototyping tools that allow you to experiment with color schemes and typography before implementing them in your app's design. These tools enable you to visualize how different choices impact the overall look and feel.

6. Accessibility Considerations

Pay close attention to accessibility guidelines, such as contrast ratios and font size recommendations, to ensure that your app is usable by individuals with varying visual abilities.

7. Localization

Consider how your color choices and typography may need to adapt for different languages and writing systems. Some fonts may not support all characters required for various languages.

8. User Feedback and Iteration

Regularly collect user feedback regarding color and typography preferences. Be open to making adjustments based on user insights and preferences.

In summary, color theory and typography are powerful tools in UI/UX design that can influence user perception and engagement. By carefully selecting color palettes, fonts, and maintaining consistency, you can create visually appealing and user-friendly interfaces that resonate with your target audience.

Section 15.5: Creating an Intuitive User Flow

Creating an intuitive user flow is paramount in ensuring a positive user experience within your app. The user flow defines the path users take to accomplish their goals and interact with your app's features. In this section, we'll explore techniques to design a user-friendly and intuitive flow within your mobile application.

1. Understand Your Users

Before designing a user flow, it's crucial to understand your target audience and their needs. Conduct user research, create user personas, and gather feedback to gain insights into your users' preferences and behaviors.

2. Define Clear Goals

Identify the primary goals users want to achieve when using your app. These goals will serve as the foundation for your user flow design. Common goals include signing up, making a purchase, or accessing specific content.

3. Map Out User Journeys

Create user journey maps that outline the steps users take to achieve their goals. Visualizing these journeys helps identify potential pain points and opportunities for improvement.

4. Simplify Navigation

Simplicity is key to an intuitive user flow. Minimize the number of steps required to accomplish a task and ensure that navigation is straightforward. Use clear and concise labels for buttons and menu items.

5. Use Visual Cues

Incorporate visual cues such as icons, buttons, and progress indicators to guide users through the app. These cues help users understand where they are in the process and what actions they can take.

6. Consistent Layout and Design

Maintain a consistent layout and design across your app to reduce cognitive load. Users should easily recognize common elements and interactions, enhancing their understanding of how to use the app.

7. Feedback and Confirmation

Provide immediate feedback when users perform actions. For example, display a success message after a form submission or show a loading indicator during a process. Confirmation and feedback reassure users that their actions are being processed.

8. Error Handling

Anticipate user errors and provide clear error messages that guide users on how to rectify issues. Avoid generic error messages and instead offer specific instructions.

```swift
func validateInput() {

// Check if user input is valid

if inputIsInvalid {

showError(message: "Please enter a valid email address.")

} else {

// Continue with the next step

}

}

func showError(message: String) {

// Display an error message to the user
```

```
let alertController = UIAlertController(title: "Error", message:
message, preferredStyle: .alert)

alertController.addAction(UIAlertAction(title: "OK", style:
.default, handler: nil))

present(alertController, animated: true, completion: nil)

}
```

9. User Testing

Conduct usability testing with real users to evaluate the effectiveness of your user flow. Collect feedback and make iterative improvements based on user insights.

10. Optimize for Mobile

Consider the unique characteristics of mobile devices, such as smaller screens and touch interactions. Ensure that your user flow is optimized for mobile use and provides a seamless experience on various screen sizes.

11. Onboarding

If your app requires user onboarding, keep it concise and informative. Walk users through essential features and functionalities to get them started quickly.

12. Analytics and Monitoring

Implement analytics tools to track user interactions and identify bottlenecks or drop-off points in your user flow. Continuous monitoring allows you to make data-driven improvements.

13. Personalization

Consider incorporating personalization features that tailor the user experience based on user preferences and behavior. Personalized content and recommendations can enhance user engagement.

In conclusion, creating an intuitive user flow is a critical aspect of mobile app design. By understanding your users, defining clear goals, simplifying navigation, providing feedback, and conducting user testing, you can ensure that users can easily accomplish their tasks and have a positive experience while using your app.

Chapter 16: Security and Privacy in Apps

Section 16.1: Implementing Security Best Practices

Security is of paramount importance when developing mobile applications. Users trust that their data and interactions are kept safe from prying eyes and malicious actors. In this section, we will explore the fundamental best practices for implementing security in your iOS apps.

1. Data Encryption

One of the foundational security measures is data encryption. iOS provides robust encryption capabilities through its Core Data and Keychain services. You should encrypt sensitive data at rest and during transmission to protect it from unauthorized access. Apple's Security.framework provides tools for encryption and decryption.

Here's a snippet demonstrating encryption using SecKeyEncrypt:

// Encrypt data using a public key

```swift
func encryptData(data: Data, publicKey: SecKey) throws -> Data {

var error: Unmanaged<CFError>?

guard let encryptedData = SecKeyEncrypt(publicKey, .PKCS1, data as CFData, &error) as Data? else {

throw error!.takeRetainedValue() as Error

}

return encryptedData

}
```

2. Secure Network Communications

When your app communicates with a server or external services, it's crucial to use secure communication protocols like HTTPS. You should also implement certificate pinning to ensure that your app only communicates with trusted servers. Apple's URLSession makes it easy to configure secure network requests.

```swift
let url = URL(string: "https://example.com/api/data")!

let session = URLSession(configuration: .default)

let task = session.dataTask(with: url) { data, response, error in

if let error = error {

// Handle network error

return

}

// Process the received data securely
```

```
}
task.resume()
```

3. Authentication and Authorization

Implement robust authentication and authorization mechanisms in your app to ensure that only authorized users can access specific features or data. Apple's AuthenticationServices framework simplifies the integration of Sign in with Apple, which provides a secure and user-friendly authentication method.

4. Data Storage

Sensitive data, such as user credentials or personal information, should be securely stored. iOS provides the Keychain Services API for secure storage of sensitive information. Avoid storing sensitive data in user defaults or plain text files.

5. Regular Security Audits

Regularly audit your app's security by conducting penetration testing and code reviews. Look for vulnerabilities and address them promptly. Security is an ongoing process, and staying proactive is essential to keep your app secure.

6. Stay Informed

Stay updated with the latest security threats and vulnerabilities in the iOS ecosystem. Apple releases security updates and guidelines regularly. Ensure that your app complies with these guidelines and promptly applies security updates.

In conclusion, implementing security best practices is crucial to building trust with your users and protecting their data. By following these guidelines and staying vigilant, you can create iOS apps that prioritize security and privacy.

Remember that security is a multifaceted topic, and it's essential to consider all aspects of your app's architecture and functionality to ensure a robust defense against potential threats.

Section 16.2: Data Encryption and Secure Storage

Data encryption and secure storage are critical aspects of ensuring the confidentiality and integrity of sensitive information in your iOS apps. In this section, we will delve into the techniques and best practices for encrypting and securely storing data.

1. Keychain Services

The Keychain Services API is a secure and convenient way to store sensitive data such as passwords, encryption keys, and tokens. The iOS Keychain ensures that data is encrypted and protected, even if the device is compromised.

Here's an example of how to securely store and retrieve a password in the Keychain:

```swift
import Security

func savePasswordToKeychain(password: String, account: String) {

if let passwordData = password.data(using: .utf8) {

let query: [CFString: Any] = [
```

```swift
    kSecClass: kSecClassGenericPassword,

    kSecAttrAccount: account,

    kSecValueData: passwordData

    ]

    let status = SecItemAdd(query as CFDictionary, nil)

    if status != errSecSuccess {

    // Handle error

    }

    }

    }

func getPasswordFromKeychain(account: String) -> String? {

    let query: [CFString: Any] = [

    kSecClass: kSecClassGenericPassword,

    kSecAttrAccount: account,

    kSecReturnData: kCFBooleanTrue as Any

    ]

    var result: AnyObject?

    let status = SecItemCopyMatching(query as CFDictionary, &result)

    if status == errSecSuccess, let data = result as? Data {

    return String(data: data, encoding: .utf8)
```

```
}

return nil

}
```

2. File-Based Encryption

To protect data at rest, consider enabling file-based encryption for sensitive files. iOS provides a Data Protection API that allows you to specify the level of protection for files.

```
let fileURL = URL(fileURLWithPath: "path/to/sensitive/data.txt")

do {

try              FileManager.default.setAttributes([.protectionKey:
FileProtectionType.complete], ofItemAtPath: fileURL.path)

} catch {

// Handle error

}
```

3. Data Transmission

When transmitting sensitive data over the network, always use secure protocols like HTTPS. Ensure that your app supports the latest security standards and uses secure transport configurations.

4. Regular Data Purging

Implement a data retention policy and regularly purge sensitive data that is no longer needed. This reduces the potential impact of data breaches.

5. Secure Data Backup

Consider disabling the backup of sensitive data to iCloud by marking files or directories as non-backup items. This prevents sensitive data from being stored in unencrypted iCloud backups.

let fileURL = URL(fileURLWithPath: "path/to/sensitive/data.txt")

do {

try fileURL.setResourceValues([.isExcludedFromBackupKey: **true**])

} **catch** {

// Handle error

}

6. Strong Authentication

Require strong user authentication, such as biometrics or passcodes, to access sensitive data within your app. Use the iOS Face ID and Touch ID APIs for biometric authentication.

By following these best practices for data encryption and secure storage, you can enhance the security of your iOS app and protect user data from potential threats and vulnerabilities. Always stay informed about the latest security updates and guidelines provided by Apple to ensure your app remains secure.

Section 16.3: Network Security and API Protection

Network security is a paramount concern when developing iOS apps, especially when your app communicates with remote servers and APIs. In this section, we'll explore strategies and best practices for enhancing network security and protecting your app's interactions with external services.

1. Secure Communication

When your app communicates with a remote server or API, it's essential to ensure that the communication is secure. Use HTTPS (Hypertext Transfer Protocol Secure) for all network requests to encrypt data in transit. You should never transmit sensitive information over HTTP, which is not secure.

```swift
import Alamofire // or URLSession

let url = URL(string: "https://api.example.com/data")!

// Make a secure HTTPS request

AF.request(url, method: .get)

.responseJSON { response in

switch response.result {

case .success(let value):

// Handle the response data

case .failure(let error):

// Handle the error

}

}
```

2. Certificate Pinning

Implement certificate pinning to enhance security. This involves validating that the server's SSL/TLS certificate matches a known certificate or public key embedded in your app. It helps protect against man-in-the-middle attacks.

```swift
import Alamofire // or URLSession

let url = URL(string: "https://api.example.com/data")!

// Define the expected public key or certificate

let publicKeyHash = "AB12CD34EF...".data(using: .utf8)!

let serverTrustManager = ServerTrustManager(evaluators: [

url.host!:              PinnedCertificatesTrustEvaluator(certificates: [publicKeyHash])

])

let session = Session(serverTrustManager: serverTrustManager)

// Make a request using the configured session

session.request(url, method: .get)

.responseJSON { response in

switch response.result {

case .success(let value):
// Handle the response data

case .failure(let error):
// Handle the error
```

```
}

}
```

3. OAuth and API Tokens

When accessing third-party APIs, consider using OAuth for authentication and authorization. OAuth allows your app to access resources on behalf of a user without exposing their credentials. Store API tokens securely and use them in requests.

4. Rate Limiting and Access Control

Implement rate limiting on your API endpoints to prevent abuse and protect against Distributed Denial of Service (DDoS) attacks. Additionally, enforce access control rules to ensure that only authorized users can access specific resources.

5. Data Validation

Always validate data received from external sources, such as APIs, before processing it. Validate input data to prevent security vulnerabilities like SQL injection and cross-site scripting (XSS) attacks.

6. API Versioning

When developing and maintaining APIs, use versioning to ensure backward compatibility with existing clients. This helps prevent unexpected changes from breaking your app's functionality.

7. Security Headers

Consider using security headers in your app's web requests. Headers like Content Security Policy (CSP) and X-Content-Type-Options can help mitigate common web security vulnerabilities.

By incorporating these network security best practices and staying updated on the latest security threats and solutions, you can significantly reduce the risk of security breaches and ensure the safety of your users' data during network interactions.

Section 16.4: Privacy Policies and User Data

Protecting user privacy is a fundamental aspect of iOS app development. Users expect their personal data to be handled with care and in compliance with privacy regulations. In this section, we'll explore the importance of privacy policies and how to handle user data responsibly.

1. Privacy Policy

A privacy policy is a legal document that informs users about how your app collects, uses, and protects their personal data. It's essential to have a clear and comprehensive privacy policy that complies with applicable laws and regulations, such as the General Data Protection Regulation (GDPR) in Europe or the California Consumer Privacy Act (CCPA) in the United States.

2. Transparency

Be transparent about the data you collect and why you collect it. Your app should provide clear explanations to users regarding the types of data you gather, how you use it, and whether you share it with third parties. Transparency builds trust and helps users make informed decisions.

3. Data Minimization

Adopt a data minimization approach. Only collect the data that is necessary for your app's functionality. Avoid requesting excessive permissions or collecting information that is unrelated to your app's core features.

4. Consent

Obtain explicit consent from users before collecting or processing their personal data. Implement a consent mechanism that allows users to opt in or opt out of data collection. Consent should be freely given, informed, specific, and revocable.

5. Data Security

Protect user data with robust security measures. Use encryption to secure data both in transit and at rest. Implement access controls to ensure that only authorized personnel can access user data. Regularly audit and test your app's security.

6. Data Retention

Define clear policies for data retention and deletion. Delete user data that is no longer necessary for your app's functionality. Communicate these policies in your privacy policy.

7. User Rights

Respect user rights concerning their data. Provide mechanisms for users to access, modify, or delete their personal information. Respond promptly to user requests related to their data.

8. Third-Party Services

If your app integrates with third-party services or SDKs (Software Development Kits), ensure that these services also comply with privacy regulations. Review their privacy policies and data handling practices.

9. Regular Updates

Keep your privacy policy up to date. As your app evolves and regulations change, review and revise your privacy policy accordingly. Notify users of any significant changes.

10. Compliance

Understand and comply with privacy regulations applicable to your app's target audience. Seek legal counsel if needed to ensure compliance with complex regulations.

Failure to prioritize user privacy can result in legal consequences, reputational damage, and loss of user trust. By implementing these best practices and maintaining a commitment to user privacy, you can create a positive and secure user experience while mitigating privacy-related risks.

Section 16.5: Avoiding Common Security Pitfalls

Security is a paramount concern in app development. Failing to address common security pitfalls can lead to vulnerabilities, data breaches, and compromised user trust. In this section, we'll explore some of the common security pitfalls and how to avoid them.

1. Insecure Data Storage

Storing sensitive data like passwords or API keys in plaintext is a major security risk. Instead, use secure storage mechanisms provided by iOS, such as the Keychain Services, to store sensitive information securely. These mechanisms encrypt data and protect it from unauthorized access.

```swift
// Storing a password in Keychain

let password = "superSecretPassword"

let passwordData = password.data(using: .utf8)!

let query: [String: Any] = [

kSecClass as String: kSecClassGenericPassword,

kSecAttrAccount as String: "userAccount",

kSecValueData as String: passwordData

]

let status = SecItemAdd(query as CFDictionary, nil)
```

2. Lack of Input Validation

Failing to validate user inputs can lead to security vulnerabilities like SQL injection or Cross-Site Scripting (XSS) attacks. Always validate and sanitize user inputs before processing them. Use parameterized queries when interacting with databases to prevent SQL injection.

```swift
// Parameterized query to prevent SQL injection

let userInput = "userInput"

let query = "SELECT * FROM users WHERE username = ?"
```

```
let statement = try db.prepare(query)

let rows = try statement.run(userInput)
```

3. Inadequate Authentication

Implement strong user authentication mechanisms to prevent unauthorized access to sensitive features or data. Use technologies like OAuth, OpenID Connect, or Apple's Sign In with Apple to ensure secure authentication.

```
// Authenticating a user with OAuth

func authenticateWithOAuth() {

// Implement OAuth authentication flow

}
```

4. Insufficient Authorization

Ensure that users have appropriate permissions to access different parts of your app. Implement role-based access control (RBAC) or attribute-based access control (ABAC) to manage authorization.

```
// Checking user permissions

if user.hasPermission(.writeData) {

// Allow data modification

} else {

// Deny access

}
```

5. Unhandled Errors

Failing to handle errors properly can expose sensitive information or lead to unexpected behavior. Always implement robust error handling and logging to capture and respond to errors gracefully.

```swift
// Error handling and logging

do {

try performSecureOperation()

} catch let error {

// Log the error and handle it appropriately

print("Error: \(error.localizedDescription)")

}
```

6. Lack of Encryption

Ensure that data transmitted over the network is encrypted using secure protocols like HTTPS. Avoid transmitting sensitive data over unencrypted channels.

```swift
// Making an HTTPS request

let url = URL(string: "https://example.com/api/data")!

let task = URLSession.shared.dataTask(with: url) { data, response, error in

// Handle the response securely

}

task.resume()
```

7. Delayed Patching

Failing to promptly apply security patches and updates to your app can leave it vulnerable to known exploits. Stay up to date with security advisories and release updates as needed.

Addressing these common security pitfalls and staying informed about emerging threats and best practices is crucial for building secure iOS applications that protect user data and maintain user trust.

Chapter 17: Advanced Networking

Section 17.1: Deep Dive into HTTP and WebSockets

Networking is a fundamental aspect of many iOS applications, and a deep understanding of the underlying protocols is crucial for building robust and efficient networked apps. In this section, we will take a comprehensive look at HTTP (Hypertext Transfer Protocol) and WebSockets, which are widely used in modern iOS development for communication between clients and servers.

HTTP Basics

HTTP is the foundation of data communication on the World Wide Web. It is an application layer protocol that facilitates the transfer of data between a client (typically a web browser or mobile app) and a web server. Key aspects of HTTP include:

- **Request-Response Model:** HTTP operates on a request-response model, where a client sends an HTTP request to a server, and the server responds with the requested data or an error message.

- **Stateless:** HTTP is a stateless protocol, meaning each request from a client to the server must contain all the information needed to understand and process the request. The server does not maintain any session state between requests.

- **Methods:** HTTP defines various request methods, such as GET (retrieve data), POST (submit data), PUT (update data), DELETE (remove data), etc.

- **Status Codes:** HTTP responses include status codes that indicate the outcome of the request. For example, a status code of 200 means a successful request, while 404 indicates that the requested resource was not found.

- **Headers:** HTTP requests and responses can contain headers to convey additional information. Common headers include Content-Type (specifying the format of the data), Authorization (for authentication), and Cookie (for maintaining session state).

Making HTTP Requests in iOS

In iOS, you can make HTTP requests using various libraries and APIs. One commonly used approach is by utilizing URLSession, which provides a high-level API for making HTTP requests asynchronously. Here's a basic example of making a GET request:

```swift
let url = URL(string: "https://api.example.com/data")!

let task = URLSession.shared.dataTask(with: url) { data, response, error in

if let error = error {

print("Error: \(error.localizedDescription)")

return

}

if let data = data {

// Process the received data here

}
```

```
}

task.resume()
```

WebSockets

WebSockets provide full-duplex communication channels over a single TCP connection, making them suitable for real-time applications. Unlike HTTP, which follows a request-response model, WebSockets allow bidirectional communication between the client and server.

Key features of WebSockets include:

- **Low Latency:** WebSockets are designed for low-latency communication, making them ideal for applications like chat, online gaming, and collaborative tools.

- **Bi-directional:** Both the client and server can initiate communication, allowing for real-time updates from either end.

- **Efficient:** WebSockets have less overhead compared to HTTP, as they don't require the headers associated with each HTTP request.

- **Persistent Connection:** WebSockets maintain a persistent connection until either the client or server decides to close it.

Using WebSockets in iOS

To use WebSockets in iOS, you can leverage third-party libraries like Starscream or SwiftWebSocket. These libraries provide abstractions to handle WebSocket connections and events efficiently.

Here's a simplified example using the Starscream library:

```swift
import Starscream

let socket = WebSocket(url: URL(string: "wss://websocket.example.com/socket")!)

socket.onConnect = {

print("WebSocket is connected")

}

socket.onDisconnect = { (error: Error?) in

print("WebSocket is disconnected with error: \(error?.localizedDescription ?? "")")

}

socket.onText = { (text: String) in

print("Received text: \(text)")

}

socket.connect()
```

In this section, we've covered the basics of HTTP and WebSockets in iOS development. Understanding these protocols is crucial for building applications that communicate effectively with remote servers and provide real-time features to users. In the following sections, we'll delve deeper into other aspects of advanced networking, including implementing RESTful APIs, working with GraphQL, optimizing network calls, and addressing security considerations.

Section 17.2: Implementing RESTful APIs

REST (Representational State Transfer) is an architectural style for designing networked applications. RESTful APIs (Application Programming Interfaces) adhere to REST principles and have become a standard for building web services that can be consumed by various clients, including iOS apps. In this section, we'll explore the fundamentals of RESTful APIs and how to implement them in iOS development.

Key Principles of REST

REST is based on several key principles:

1. **Stateless:** Like HTTP, REST is stateless, meaning each request from a client to a server must contain all the information needed to understand and process the request. The server does not maintain any session state between requests.

2. **Resources:** In REST, resources are represented as URLs (Uniform Resource Locators). Resources can be anything that can be named, such as objects, data, or services. For example, in an e-commerce app, products could be represented as resources.

3. **HTTP Methods:** RESTful APIs use HTTP methods to perform actions on resources. Common HTTP methods include GET (retrieve data), POST (create new data), PUT (update data), DELETE (remove data), and more.

4. **Stateless Communication:** Each request from the client to the server should be stateless and contain all the necessary information. The server should not rely on information from previous requests.

Making RESTful Requests in iOS

To make RESTful requests in iOS, you can use libraries like Alamofire or the built-in URLSession. Alamofire is a popular Swift-based HTTP networking library that simplifies the process of making HTTP requests.

Here's an example of making a GET request using Alamofire:

```swift
import Alamofire

let url = "https://api.example.com/products"

AF.request(url, method: .get)

.validate()

.responseJSON { response in

switch response.result {

case .success(let value):

// Handle successful response and parse JSON data

print("Response JSON: \(value)")

case .failure(let error):

// Handle error

print("Error: \(error)")

}

}
```

In this example, we use Alamofire to send a GET request to retrieve a list of products from the server. The response can be processed and parsed based on the expected data format, typically in JSON or XML.

Handling Authentication

Many RESTful APIs require authentication to access protected resources. Common authentication methods include API keys, OAuth 2.0, and token-based authentication.

For example, if an API requires an API key, you can include it in the request headers:

```swift
import Alamofire

let url = "https://api.example.com/protected-resource"

let apiKey = "your-api-key"

let headers: HTTPHeaders = [

"Authorization": "Bearer \(apiKey)"

]

AF.request(url, method: .get, headers: headers)

.validate()

.responseJSON { response in

// Handle response and authentication

}
```

In this case, we include the API key in the Authorization header of the request.

Error Handling and Status Codes

When working with RESTful APIs, it's important to handle different HTTP status codes. Common status codes include:

- 200: OK (successful response)

- 201: Created (resource successfully created)

- 204: No Content (successful request with no response)

- 400: Bad Request (invalid request)

- 401: Unauthorized (authentication required)

- 403: Forbidden (access denied)

- 404: Not Found (resource not found)

- 500: Internal Server Error (server error)

Handling these status codes appropriately in your iOS app allows you to provide meaningful feedback to users and implement error recovery mechanisms.

In summary, RESTful APIs are a standard way to design and implement web services that can be easily consumed by iOS applications. Understanding the principles of REST, making HTTP requests using libraries like Alamofire, handling authentication, and managing different HTTP status codes are essential skills for iOS developers working with web APIs. In the following sections, we'll explore more advanced topics in iOS networking, such as working with GraphQL, optimizing network calls, and addressing security considerations.

Section 17.3: Working with GraphQL in iOS

GraphQL is a query language for APIs and a runtime for executing those queries by the server. Unlike traditional REST APIs, GraphQL allows clients to request only the specific data they need, reducing over-fetching or under-fetching of data. In this section, we'll explore how to work with GraphQL in iOS development.

Understanding GraphQL

GraphQL revolves around the concept of a schema, which defines the data types and operations that can be performed. A GraphQL schema consists of types, queries, and mutations.

- **Types:** Types define the structure of data. Scalar types (e.g., Int, String) represent atomic values, while object types define complex structures.

- **Queries:** Queries define the operations that clients can perform to retrieve data. Clients specify the fields they need in a query, and the server responds with data that matches the query structure.

- **Mutations:** Mutations are similar to queries but are used for modifying data. Clients can send mutations to create, update, or delete data on the server.

Setting Up GraphQL in iOS

To work with GraphQL in iOS, you can use various libraries like Apollo Client or the built-in URLSession for making HTTP POST requests.

Here's a basic example of making a GraphQL query using URLSession:

```swift
import Foundation

let graphQLURL = URL(string: "https://api.example.com/graphql")!

let query = """
{
user(id: "123") {
id
name
email
}
}
"""

var request = URLRequest(url: graphQLURL)

request.httpMethod = "POST"

request.addValue("application/json", forHTTPHeaderField: "Content-Type")

request.httpBody = try? JSONSerialization.data(withJSONObject: ["query": query], options: [])

let task = URLSession.shared.dataTask(with: request) { data, response, error in
if let data = data {
// Parse and handle GraphQL response
```

```
} else if let error = error {

// Handle error

}

}

task.resume()
```

In this example, we send a GraphQL query as a JSON payload to the server and handle the response accordingly.

Working with GraphQL Clients

GraphQL clients like Apollo Client for iOS provide a more convenient way to work with GraphQL APIs. These clients generate Swift code from your GraphQL schema, making it type-safe and reducing the risk of runtime errors.

To use Apollo Client, you typically follow these steps:

1. Define your GraphQL schema and queries in a .graphql or .graphqls file.
2. Use Apollo's code generation tool to generate Swift types and queries from your schema.
3. Execute queries and mutations using the generated Swift code.

Apollo Client ensures that your queries conform to the schema, provides autocompletion, and handles caching and data normalization.

Handling Authentication

Similar to RESTful APIs, GraphQL APIs may require authentication. You can include authentication tokens or headers in your GraphQL requests, just as you would with REST.

Error Handling and Optimizations

When working with GraphQL, it's crucial to handle errors and optimize queries to avoid over-fetching data. GraphQL allows clients to specify exactly what data they need, but it's the responsibility of the client to make efficient queries.

In summary, GraphQL is a powerful way to retrieve data in a more efficient and flexible manner than traditional REST APIs. By understanding GraphQL concepts, setting up GraphQL in your iOS app, working with GraphQL clients, handling authentication, and optimizing queries, you can build efficient and responsive iOS applications that communicate effectively with your backend services.

Section 17.4: Optimizing Network Calls

Efficient network communication is crucial for the performance of your iOS app. In this section, we'll explore various strategies and best practices to optimize network calls in your iOS applications.

1. Batch Requests

Reducing the number of network requests can significantly improve performance. Consider batching multiple requests into a single call when possible. This reduces overhead and latency, especially when dealing with REST APIs.

2. Pagination

When dealing with large datasets, implement pagination instead of fetching all data at once. Pagination allows you to load and display data incrementally, improving app responsiveness. You can use GraphQL's built-in pagination features or implement your pagination logic with RESTful APIs.

3. Caching

Caching responses locally can dramatically reduce the need for network requests. iOS provides built-in caching mechanisms like URLCache for HTTP responses. You can configure caching policies and expiration times to control how data is cached.

4. Use Compression

Enable compression for data transferred over the network. Many APIs support compression formats like gzip or Brotli. Compressed data reduces bandwidth usage and speeds up downloads.

5. Throttling and Debouncing

Throttling and debouncing are techniques to control the frequency of network requests. Throttling limits the number of requests per unit of time, while debouncing ensures that a request is made only after a pause in user activity. These techniques prevent excessive network traffic.

6. Background Fetch

Fetch data in the background when the app is not in use to keep content up to date. You can use Background Fetch APIs to schedule periodic updates. Be mindful of battery usage and network constraints.

7. Use Content Delivery Networks (CDNs)

If your app serves media files or other large assets, consider using a Content Delivery Network (CDN). CDNs distribute content to edge servers worldwide, reducing latency and improving download speeds for users.

8. Error Handling

Implement robust error handling to gracefully handle network issues. Provide meaningful error messages and give users options to retry or take appropriate actions. Use reachability checks to detect network availability.

9. Avoid Over-fetching

With GraphQL, clients request only the data they need, reducing over-fetching. However, with REST, it's essential to design APIs that provide the right level of granularity to prevent fetching unnecessary data.

10. Monitor Network Performance

Use network monitoring tools like Charles Proxy or network profiling in Xcode Instruments to analyze network traffic. Identify bottlenecks and areas for improvement in your app's network communication.

11. Background Transfer Service

For long-running uploads or downloads, consider using the Background Transfer Service provided by iOS. This service allows your app to continue transfers even when the app is in the background or terminated.

12. Minimize Redundant Requests

Avoid making duplicate requests for the same data. Implement caching or check if data is already available before initiating a network request.

13. HTTP/2 and HTTP/3

Ensure that your server supports modern HTTP protocols like HTTP/2 or HTTP/3. These protocols offer improved performance, multiplexing, and reduced latency compared to HTTP/1.1.

14. Optimize Images

If your app deals with images, use image optimization techniques. Compress images appropriately, choose the right format (JPEG, PNG, WebP), and consider lazy loading to defer image loading until they are visible.

By implementing these network optimization strategies, you can ensure that your iOS app communicates efficiently with backend services, providing a smooth and responsive user experience while minimizing data usage and latency.

Section 17.5: Security Considerations in Networking

When developing iOS applications that communicate over the network, ensuring security is paramount. In this section, we'll explore various security considerations and best practices for network communication in iOS apps.

1. Transport Layer Security (TLS)

Always use Transport Layer Security (TLS) to encrypt data in transit. Ensure that your app's network requests use HTTPS rather than HTTP. iOS enforces App Transport Security (ATS) by default, which requires network connections to use secure protocols.

```swift
// Example of an HTTPS request in Swift

let url = URL(string: "https://example.com/api/data")!

let task = URLSession.shared.dataTask(with: url) { data, response, error in

// Handle the response

}

task.resume()
```

2. Certificate Pinning

Implement certificate pinning to enhance security. This practice involves associating a specific server's SSL certificate with your app. If the certificate doesn't match during a connection, the app should reject the connection, even if the certificate is valid. This guards against man-in-the-middle attacks.

```swift
// Example of certificate pinning in Swift

let serverCertificateHash = "your_certificate_hash"

let pinnedCertificates = Bundle.main.certificates

if pinnedCertificates.contains(serverCertificateHash) {

// Proceed with the connection
```

```
} else {

// Reject the connection

}
```

3. Secure Credential Storage

Store sensitive information, such as API keys and tokens, securely in the Keychain. The Keychain provides a secure and encrypted storage mechanism for credentials, ensuring they are not easily accessible by malicious actors.

```
// Example of storing and retrieving data in the Keychain

let keychain = Keychain(service: "com.yourapp.api")

keychain["apiToken"] = "your_api_token"

let storedToken = keychain["apiToken"]
```

4. Secure Coding Practices

Follow secure coding practices to prevent common vulnerabilities like SQL injection, cross-site scripting (XSS), and remote code execution. Always validate and sanitize user input before using it in network requests.

5. OAuth and OAuth 2.0

When implementing authentication, consider using OAuth or OAuth 2.0 for secure user authorization. These protocols provide robust mechanisms for authentication and access control.

6. Two-Factor Authentication (2FA)

Encourage or require users to enable two-factor authentication (2FA) for their accounts. 2FA adds an additional layer of security, making it more challenging for unauthorized users to access sensitive data.

7. Rate Limiting

Implement rate limiting on your API endpoints to prevent abuse and protect against Distributed Denial of Service (DDoS) attacks. Rate limiting restricts the number of requests a user or IP address can make within a specific timeframe.

8. Data Validation and Sanitization

Validate and sanitize data received from external sources, including API responses. Protect your app from malicious data that could exploit vulnerabilities.

9. Logging and Monitoring

Implement robust logging and monitoring for network requests and responses. In case of security incidents or anomalies, logs can help diagnose and respond to potential threats promptly.

10. Security Audits

Regularly conduct security audits and penetration testing to identify and address vulnerabilities in your app's network communication. Engage security experts or firms to perform comprehensive assessments.

11. Privacy Policies and User Consent

Clearly communicate your app's data handling practices to users and obtain their consent for data collection and usage, in compliance with privacy regulations like GDPR or CCPA.

By incorporating these security considerations and best practices into your iOS app's network communication, you can enhance the protection of sensitive data, mitigate security risks, and build trust with your users, ensuring a secure and safe user experience.

Chapter 18: Monetization Strategies

Section 18.1: Overview of App Monetization

Monetizing your iOS app is a crucial aspect of app development. While some developers create apps purely for the joy of building, many others seek to generate revenue from their hard work. In this section, we'll provide an overview of app monetization strategies and discuss various approaches you can consider.

1. Freemium Model

The freemium model allows users to download your app for free and offers premium features or content through in-app purchases (IAPs). It's a popular strategy that attracts a wide user base and generates revenue from a subset of users who opt for premium offerings.

```swift
// Example of implementing an in-app purchase in Swift

func purchasePremiumContent() {

if SKPaymentQueue.canMakePayments() {

let productID = "com.yourapp.premium"
```

```swift
let payment = SKPayment(product: productID)

SKPaymentQueue.default().add(payment)

}

}
```

2. In-App Advertising

Integrating ads within your app is another common monetization method. You can partner with ad networks like Google AdMob or Facebook Audience Network to display ads to users. Revenue is generated through ad impressions, clicks, or user interactions.

// Example of displaying an ad banner in Swift

```swift
let adView = GADBannerView(adSize: kGADAdSizeBanner)

adView.adUnitID = "your_ad_unit_id"

adView.rootViewController = self

let request = GADRequest()

adView.load(request)
```

3. Subscriptions

Offering subscription-based access to your app's content or features can provide a steady stream of revenue. Subscriptions can be monthly, yearly, or based on other intervals. Ensure you provide compelling content or functionality to justify the recurring cost.

// Example of managing subscriptions in Swift

```
let subscriptionManager = SubscriptionManager()

if subscriptionManager.isSubscribed() {

// Grant access to premium content

} else {

// Show subscription options

}
```

4. Paid Apps

Releasing a paid app means users must purchase it upfront to access any features or content. While this approach can generate revenue quickly, it may limit the number of users willing to pay. Ensure your app delivers significant value to justify the price.

```
// Example of setting the app's price in the App Store Connect

// Users must purchase the app to download and use it.
```

5. Sponsorships and Partnerships

Collaborating with sponsors or partners can be a lucrative monetization strategy. This involves promoting third-party products, services, or brands within your app. Ensure partnerships align with your app's target audience and don't compromise the user experience.

6. Affiliate Marketing

You can earn commissions by including affiliate links or referral codes within your app. When users make purchases through these links, you receive a portion of the revenue. Carefully select affiliate programs relevant to your app's content.

7. Donations and Crowdfunding

Some developers rely on the goodwill of their users and offer donation options within their apps. Alternatively, crowdfunding platforms like Patreon or Kickstarter can help fund ongoing development.

8. Data Licensing

If your app generates valuable data, consider licensing it to other businesses or developers. Data licensing can be a significant revenue source, especially if your app collects unique or specialized data.

9. Cross-Promotion

Promote your other apps or products within your existing apps. Cross-promotion can help drive users to your different offerings, expanding your overall user base and revenue potential.

10. E-commerce Integration

If your app aligns with e-commerce, consider integrating shopping functionality. You can earn commissions on sales made through your app or charge businesses for listing their products.

Choosing the right monetization strategy depends on your app's niche, target audience, and goals. In many cases, a combination of strategies may yield the best results. Continuously analyze user behavior, gather feedback, and adjust your monetization approach to maximize revenue while providing value to your users. Remember that user experience and trust are paramount, so avoid aggressive or intrusive monetization tactics that can lead to user dissatisfaction.

Section 18.2: In-App Purchases and Subscriptions

In-app purchases (IAPs) and subscriptions are popular monetization strategies for iOS apps. They allow developers to offer additional content, features, or services to users after the initial app download. This section explores in-app purchases and subscriptions in more detail, providing insights into how to implement them effectively.

Understanding In-App Purchases

In-app purchases enable users to buy digital goods or services within your app. These purchases can include items like virtual currency, additional levels, premium features, or ad removal. In iOS development, you can implement in-app purchases using Apple's StoreKit framework.

To get started with in-app purchases, follow these steps:

1. **Set Up App Store Connect**: Create in-app purchase products in your App Store Connect account. These products define what users can buy within your app. Make sure to set up necessary pricing and localization options.

2. **Integrate StoreKit**: In your Xcode project, import the StoreKit framework and set up a StoreKit observer to handle transactions.

```
import StoreKit

class IAPManager: NSObject, SKPaymentTransactionObserver {
```

// Implement the observer methods here.

}

1. **Request Products**: Use StoreKit to request product information from the App Store, allowing you to display the available in-app purchases to users.

func fetchAvailableProducts(productIDs: Set<String>) {

let productRequest = SKProductsRequest(productIdentifiers: productIDs)

productRequest.delegate = **self**

productRequest.start()

}

1. **Handle Purchases**: When a user initiates an in-app purchase, handle the purchase request and process the transaction.

func purchaseProduct(product: SKProduct) {

let payment = SKPayment(product: product)

SKPaymentQueue.**default**().add(payment)

}

1. **Restore Purchases**: Provide a way for users to restore their purchases, ensuring they can access their bought items on multiple devices or after app reinstallation.

func restorePurchases() {

```
SKPaymentQueue.default().restoreCompletedTransactions()
}
```

1. **Verify Receipts**: Implement server-side receipt verification to prevent fraudulent purchases and ensure the integrity of your in-app purchase system.

Implementing Subscriptions

Subscriptions are a recurring payment model that provides users with ongoing access to premium content or features. They are particularly suitable for apps with regularly updated content, such as news or entertainment apps.

To implement subscriptions, follow these steps:

1. **Set Up Subscription Products**: Create subscription products in App Store Connect, specifying their pricing, durations, and other relevant details.
2. **Integrate StoreKit**: Like in-app purchases, you'll need to integrate the StoreKit framework and set up an observer to handle subscription-related transactions.
3. **Display Subscription Options**: Present subscription options to users, allowing them to choose the subscription plan that suits them best.
4. **Handle Subscriptions**: When a user subscribes, make sure to process the transaction and grant access to premium content or features for the subscription duration.
5. **Handle Renewals and Expirations**: Monitor subscription status and handle renewals or expirations accordingly. StoreKit provides notifications for these events.
6. **Offer Free Trials and Promotions**: Consider offering free trial periods or promotions to attract subscribers. Apple

provides tools for setting up introductory offers.

Best Practices

When implementing in-app purchases and subscriptions, consider the following best practices:

- Clearly communicate the value of your in-app purchases and subscriptions to users.

- Ensure that the purchase process is user-friendly and straightforward.

- Offer different pricing tiers for subscriptions to accommodate a wider range of users.

- Provide the option to manage subscriptions within your app, including cancellation.

- Follow Apple's guidelines and policies regarding in-app purchases and subscriptions to avoid rejection from the App Store.

In-app purchases and subscriptions can be an effective way to monetize your app while providing users with valuable content or features. However, it's essential to strike a balance between monetization and user satisfaction to maintain a positive user experience.

Section 18.3: Advertising in Apps

Advertising is another widely used monetization strategy for mobile apps, including iOS apps. By displaying ads within your app, you can generate revenue based on user interactions with those ads. In this section, we'll explore advertising in apps, the different ad formats, and the integration process.

Types of Mobile Ads

There are various types of mobile ads that you can integrate into your iOS app. Some common ad formats include:

1. Banner Ads:

- **Description:** Banner ads are small rectangular ads that typically appear at the top or bottom of the app's user interface.

- **Integration:** You can integrate banner ads using ad network SDKs like Google AdMob or Facebook Audience Network. These SDKs provide easy-to-use components for adding banners to your app's views.

2. Interstitial Ads:

- **Description:** Interstitial ads are full-screen ads that appear at natural breaks or transitions within your app, such as between levels in a game.

- **Integration:** Interstitial ads are usually implemented as separate view controllers or modal views. Ad network SDKs offer methods to show interstitial ads when desired.

3. Rewarded Video Ads:

- **Description:** Rewarded video ads are video ads that users can choose to watch in exchange for in-app rewards, such as virtual currency or premium content.

- **Integration:** Implementing rewarded video ads involves using ad network SDKs and offering users the option to watch a video in exchange for rewards. You'll need to handle reward delivery in your app.

4. Native Ads:

- **Description:** Native ads blend seamlessly with your app's content, making them appear less intrusive. They match the style and design of your app.

- **Integration:** Native ads require custom UI implementation to ensure they fit your app's layout. Ad network SDKs provide native ad components and guidelines for proper integration.

Advertising SDKs

To display ads in your iOS app, you'll need to integrate advertising SDKs provided by ad networks. Some popular ad networks and their SDKs include:

- Google AdMob[4]: Google's advertising platform offers SDKs for banner ads, interstitial ads, rewarded video ads, and more.

---

4. https://admob.google.com/

- Facebook Audience Network: Facebook's Audience Network provides SDKs for various ad formats, including native ads.

- Chartboost[5]: Chartboost specializes in mobile game advertising and offers interstitial and rewarded video ad integration.

- Unity Ads: Unity Ads is a popular choice for game developers, offering video and rewarded video ads.

Ad Mediation

Ad mediation is a strategy to maximize your ad revenue by integrating multiple ad networks into your app. Ad mediation platforms like MoPub[6] and AdMob Mediation allow you to manage multiple ad network SDKs simultaneously. This ensures that if one ad network doesn't have an ad to display, the mediation platform can request an ad from another network, optimizing your fill rate and revenue.

Ad Targeting and User Experience

While implementing ads, it's crucial to balance revenue generation with a positive user experience. Ad targeting and frequency capping can help ensure that users see relevant ads without feeling overwhelmed by excessive advertising.

- **Targeting:** Use user data to show ads that align with users' interests and preferences. Ad networks often provide targeting options based on demographics and user behavior.

---

5. https://www.chartboost.com/

6. https://www.mopub.com/

- **Frequency Capping:** Limit the number of ads users see within a specific timeframe to prevent ad fatigue and annoyance.

- **Ad Placement:** Place ads strategically to minimize interference with the app's core functionality. Avoid intrusive ad placements that hinder the user experience.

- **Ad Quality:** Ensure that the ads displayed are of high quality and relevant to your audience. Low-quality or irrelevant ads can deter users.

- **Opt-Out Options:** Offer users the ability to opt out of personalized ads or data tracking to respect their privacy preferences.

By implementing ads thoughtfully and respecting user preferences, you can generate revenue while maintaining a positive user experience in your iOS app.

Section 18.4: Freemium vs. Paid App Strategies

When it comes to monetizing your iOS app, you have two primary options: offering a freemium app or a paid app. Each strategy has its advantages and considerations, and the choice between them depends on your app's goals, target audience, and content. In this section, we'll explore the freemium and paid app strategies, including their pros and cons.

Freemium App Strategy

A freemium app is one that is free to download and use, but it offers additional premium features or content that users can purchase. This strategy is popular in the mobile app industry and is particularly effective for apps that rely on a large user base and in-app purchases (IAPs) for revenue.

Pros of Freemium Apps:

1. **Wider User Base:** Freemium apps attract a larger user base since they are free to download, making it easier to acquire new users.
2. **Lower Entry Barrier:** Users can try out your app without any initial financial commitment, increasing the chances of downloads.
3. **Monetization Flexibility:** You can generate revenue through in-app purchases, such as unlocking advanced features, removing ads, or purchasing virtual goods.
4. **Continuous Engagement:** Users who make in-app purchases tend to be more engaged with your app over time, leading to higher lifetime value (LTV).

Cons of Freemium Apps:

1. **Monetization Challenges:** Not all users will make in-app purchases, and monetizing free users can be challenging.
2. **Balancing Act:** Striking the right balance between free and premium content is crucial to avoid alienating free users while incentivizing premium purchases.
3. **User Expectations:** Freemium apps must provide enough value for free users to remain engaged while encouraging paid transactions.
4. **Development Complexity:** Implementing and managing in-app purchases requires additional development effort and integration with payment systems.

Paid App Strategy

A paid app, on the other hand, requires users to purchase it upfront before downloading or using it. This strategy is straightforward but may limit the initial user acquisition compared to freemium apps.

Pros of Paid Apps:

1. **Immediate Revenue:** You earn revenue upfront from each download, providing a predictable income source.
2. **No Ads or In-App Purchases:** Users typically expect an ad-free and fully-featured experience without additional purchases.
3. **Focused User Base:** Users who pay for your app are likely to be more committed and engaged.
4. **Simplicity:** There's no need to implement in-app purchases or manage complex freemium strategies.

Cons of Paid Apps:

1. **Lower User Acquisition:** The barrier to entry may deter potential users, resulting in a smaller user base.
2. **Limited Reach:** Some users may hesitate to purchase apps without trying them first, reducing your potential reach.
3. **Reduced Updates Revenue:** Unlike freemium apps, paid apps may not generate additional revenue through in-app purchases or ongoing subscriptions.
4. **Competitive Market:** Users have many free alternatives, making it essential to offer a unique value proposition.

Hybrid Models

In some cases, a hybrid approach can be effective. You can offer a free version of your app (freemium) with basic features and ads to attract a wide audience. Then, provide a paid version (premium) with advanced features and an ad-free experience for users willing to pay.

Ultimately, the choice between a freemium and paid app strategy should align with your app's value proposition, target audience, and long-term goals. Careful consideration and market research can help you make an informed decision that maximizes revenue while providing value to your users.

Section 18.5: Analyzing and Maximizing Revenue Streams

After deciding on a monetization strategy for your iOS app, your journey to maximize revenue doesn't end there. It's essential to continually analyze your revenue streams, optimize your approach, and explore new opportunities for generating income. In this section, we'll delve into strategies for analyzing and maximizing revenue streams.

Revenue Analysis

Effective revenue analysis is the cornerstone of optimizing your monetization strategy. Here are some key steps to consider:

1. **Data Collection:** Implement robust analytics tools, such as Google Analytics or Firebase Analytics, to gather data on user behavior, engagement, and revenue sources.
2. **Segmentation:** Segment your user base to gain insights into how different user groups interact with your app and

generate revenue. Understanding user demographics, locations, and preferences can help tailor your strategy.

3. **Conversion Funnel:** Track the user journey from app installation to revenue generation. Identify drop-off points in the conversion funnel and optimize those areas to increase conversion rates.

4. **A/B Testing:** Experiment with different monetization methods, pricing models, or ad placements through A/B testing. Analyze the results to determine what works best for your audience.

5. **Lifetime Value (LTV):** Calculate the LTV of your users to understand the long-term revenue potential. Focus on retaining and engaging high-LTV users.

Ad Revenue Optimization

If your app relies on advertising as a revenue source, consider these optimization strategies:

1. **Ad Mediation:** Use ad mediation platforms like AdMob to maximize ad revenue by selecting the most profitable ad networks for your app.

2. **Ad Placement:** Experiment with ad placement to find the most effective positions without compromising the user experience. Common locations include interstitial ads between levels or banners at the bottom of the screen.

3. **Ad Formats:** Offer a variety of ad formats, such as video ads, native ads, and rewarded ads, to cater to different user preferences and maximize eCPM (effective cost per mille).

4. **Frequency Capping:** Limit the frequency of ads to prevent ad fatigue and maintain user engagement. Be mindful not to overwhelm users with too many ads.

In-App Purchases (IAPs)

For freemium apps with in-app purchases, consider these strategies:

1. **Value Proposition:** Clearly communicate the value of in-app purchases to users. Show how premium features or items enhance their experience.
2. **Limited-Time Offers:** Create urgency by offering time-limited discounts or special offers on in-app purchases to encourage users to buy.
3. **Seasonal Promotions:** Tailor your in-app purchase promotions to seasonal events or holidays to boost sales during peak periods.
4. **Subscription Tiers:** If you offer subscription-based content, consider introducing multiple tiers with varying levels of benefits to attract a broader range of users.

Subscription Models

For apps offering subscriptions, optimizing this revenue stream is crucial:

1. **Retention Strategies:** Focus on retaining subscribers by providing regular updates, exclusive content, and features that justify the subscription cost.
2. **Trial Periods:** Offer free trial periods to allow users to experience the value of your subscription service before committing.
3. **Auto-Renewable Subscriptions:** Use auto-renewable subscription models to ensure a continuous revenue stream from loyal users.
4. **Pricing Flexibility:** Adjust subscription pricing based on user feedback, market conditions, and the perceived value of your offering.

Diversification

Exploring new revenue streams is essential for long-term sustainability:

1. **Merchandise and Merchandising:** If applicable, consider selling merchandise related to your app's content or brand.
2. **Affiliate Marketing:** Partner with relevant affiliate programs to earn commissions for driving sales or leads through your app.
3. **Sponsored Content:** Collaborate with sponsors or advertisers to incorporate sponsored content or promotions within your app.
4. **Cross-Promotion:** Promote other apps or products you own to your user base, leveraging your existing audience.
5. **Licensing and Intellectual Property:** Explore opportunities to license your app's content, characters, or technology to third parties.

Remember that revenue optimization is an ongoing process. Regularly review your strategies, adapt to market changes, and listen to user feedback to ensure your app continues to generate revenue effectively.

Chapter 19: Emerging Technologies in iOS Development

Section 19.1: Exploring Augmented Reality (AR)

Augmented Reality (AR) has gained significant attention in recent years and has found its way into various iOS applications, revolutionizing user experiences. AR technology allows developers to overlay digital content, such as 3D objects, animations, or information, onto the real-world environment seen through the device's camera. In this section, we'll explore the world of AR development on iOS.

The ARKit Framework

Apple introduced the ARKit framework, which simplifies AR app development on iOS devices. ARKit provides tools and resources for motion tracking, scene understanding, and rendering, making it easier for developers to create immersive AR experiences.

To get started with ARKit, you'll need:

1. **iOS Device:** ARKit requires an iOS device with an A9 chip or later, running iOS 11 or newer.
2. **Development Environment:** Xcode, Apple's official integrated development environment (IDE), is essential for ARKit development.

ARKit Features

1. World Tracking: ARKit allows your app to understand the real-world environment by tracking the device's motion and positioning it in 3D space. This enables stable and accurate placement of AR objects.

2. Scene Understanding: ARKit can detect horizontal planes, such as floors and tables, and provide information about their size and location. This feature is useful for anchoring virtual objects in the real world.

3. Light Estimation: ARKit considers the ambient lighting conditions and adjusts the appearance of virtual objects to make them blend seamlessly with the real environment.

4. Face Tracking: On devices with TrueDepth cameras (e.g., iPhone X and later), ARKit offers face tracking capabilities, allowing you to create engaging AR experiences involving facial expressions and animations.

Setting Up an ARKit Project

To create an ARKit project in Xcode, follow these steps:

1. Open Xcode and select "File" > "New" > "Project."
2. Choose the "Augmented Reality App" template under "iOS."
3. Configure your project settings, including its name and organization.
4. Select "Swift" as the programming language.
5. Choose the desired device for testing your AR app.
6. Click "Next" and specify a location to save your project.
7. Xcode will generate a basic ARKit project for you to build upon.

ARKit Development Resources

Apple provides comprehensive documentation and sample code to help you get started with ARKit development. Additionally, the developer community has created various tutorials and resources to assist you in creating AR experiences tailored to your app's needs.

In summary, ARKit has opened up exciting opportunities for iOS developers to create interactive and immersive augmented reality experiences. Whether you're building games, educational apps, or productivity tools, ARKit can add a new dimension to your iOS applications, providing users with innovative and engaging content.

Section 19.2: Machine Learning with CoreML

Machine learning (ML) is a transformative technology that has made its way into various domains, including iOS app development. With the Core ML framework, Apple has provided developers with a powerful tool to integrate machine learning models into their applications seamlessly. In this section, we will explore the capabilities of Core ML and how it can be leveraged in iOS development.

Introduction to Core ML

Core ML is a machine learning framework introduced by Apple, specifically designed for iOS, macOS, watchOS, and tvOS. It enables developers to integrate pre-trained machine learning models into their applications, allowing them to perform tasks such as image recognition, natural language processing, and more.

One of the significant advantages of Core ML is its efficiency. It's optimized for on-device processing, ensuring that ML tasks can be performed quickly and without relying on a network connection. This is crucial for applications that require real-time or offline ML capabilities.

Key Features of Core ML

1. Wide Range of Supported Models: Core ML supports various machine learning model types, including neural networks, decision trees, and support vector machines. This flexibility allows developers to choose the best model for their specific task.

2. On-Device Processing: With on-device processing, Core ML ensures data privacy and faster inference. User data doesn't need to be sent to remote servers, which enhances both security and performance.

3. Model Conversion Tools: Apple provides tools like Core ML Converter to convert models from popular ML libraries such as TensorFlow and scikit-learn into Core ML format, making it easier to bring existing models into your iOS app.

Integrating Core ML into Your App

To integrate Core ML into your iOS app, follow these steps:

1. **Choose or Train a Model:** Select a pre-trained model or train your custom model using ML libraries such as TensorFlow or PyTorch.
2. **Convert the Xcode:** If your model is not already in Core ML format, use conversion tools like Core ML Converter to convert it.
3. **Import the Model:** Add the Core ML model file to your Xcode project.

4. **Use Core ML in Code:** In your Swift code, you can import the Core ML framework and use the model for inference. You can pass input data and receive predictions as output.

Here's a simplified example of using a pre-trained Core ML model for image classification:

```swift
import CoreML

import Vision

// Load the Core ML model

guard let model = try? VNCoreMLModel(for: MyImageClassifier().model) else {

fatalError("Failed to load Core ML model")

}

// Create a Vision request

let request = VNCoreMLRequest(model: model) { request, error in

if let results = request.results as? [VNClassificationObservation] {

// Process classification results

for result in results {

print("\(result.identifier) (\(result.confidence * 100)%)")

}

}

}
```

// Perform image classification

let image = *// Your input image*

let handler = VNImageRequestHandler(cgImage: image.cgImage!)

try? handler.perform([request])

Resources for Core ML Development

Apple offers comprehensive documentation and resources for Core ML development, including sample code and tutorials. Additionally, the developer community has created various machine learning models and tools that can be integrated into your iOS applications. Machine learning with Core ML opens up a world of possibilities for enhancing your app's capabilities and providing innovative features to your users.

Section 19.3: Implementing Voice Recognition

Voice recognition, also known as speech recognition, is a fascinating technology that allows machines to understand and interpret spoken language. In iOS development, implementing voice recognition can lead to innovative and user-friendly applications. In this section, we will explore how to implement voice recognition in your iOS app using Apple's Speech framework.

Introduction to the Speech Framework

Apple introduced the Speech framework in iOS 10, providing developers with a straightforward way to integrate voice recognition capabilities into their applications. The Speech framework supports transcription of spoken words into text, allowing you to process voice commands or convert spoken content into readable text.

Key Features of the Speech Framework

1. Speech-to-Text Conversion: The primary feature of the Speech framework is its ability to convert spoken words into text. This enables you to capture and analyze voice input from users.

2. Offline Recognition: The Speech framework supports offline voice recognition, meaning it can process voice input without an internet connection. This is essential for applications that require real-time voice interaction.

3. Voice Control: You can use the Speech framework to create voice-controlled interfaces, allowing users to perform actions in your app through voice commands.

Implementing Voice Recognition

To implement voice recognition in your iOS app, follow these steps:

1. **Import the Speech Framework:** Start by importing the Speech framework in your Swift code.

import Speech

1. **Request User Authorization:** Before using voice recognition, you need to request user authorization. Add a usage description key to your app's Info.plist file to explain why you need access to the microphone.

<key>NSSpeechRecognitionUsageDescription</key>

<**string**>We need access to your microphone to recognize speech.</**string**>

1. **Configure and Start Recognition:** Create an instance of SFSpeechRecognizer, configure it, and request recognition.

let recognizer = SFSpeechRecognizer(locale: Locale(identifier: "en-US")) *// Change to desired locale*

let request = SFSpeechAudioBufferRecognitionRequest()

recognizer?.recognitionTask(with: request) { (result, error) **in**

if let result = result {

let recognizedText = result.bestTranscription.formattedString

// Handle the recognized text

} **else if let** error = error {

// Handle the recognition error

}

}

// Start capturing audio input

let audioEngine = AVAudioEngine()

let inputNode = audioEngine.inputNode

let recordingFormat = inputNode.outputFormat(forBus: 0)

inputNode.installTap(onBus: 0, bufferSize: 1024, format: recordingFormat) { (buffer, time) **in**

```
request.append(buffer)

}

audioEngine.prepare()

try? audioEngine.start()
```

1. **Handle Recognition Results:** As the user speaks, the recognition task provides results in real-time. You can access the recognized text from result.bestTranscription.formattedString and take appropriate actions in your app.

Use Cases for Voice Recognition

Voice recognition can be used in a variety of iOS applications, including:

- **Voice Assistants:** Create your own Siri-like voice assistant for specific tasks.

- **Transcription Apps:** Build apps that transcribe spoken content into text for notes or documents.

- **Voice Search:** Implement voice search functionality within your app.

- **Accessibility Features:** Enhance accessibility by allowing users to control your app through voice commands.

Voice recognition is a versatile technology that can significantly improve the user experience in your iOS applications. By following the steps outlined in this section, you can incorporate voice recognition into your app and open up new possibilities for user interaction.

Section 19.4: Internet of Things (IoT) Integration

The Internet of Things (IoT) is a revolutionary concept that refers to the network of interconnected physical devices, vehicles, buildings, and other objects that collect and exchange data over the internet. Integrating IoT functionality into your iOS app can enhance its capabilities and allow users to control and monitor IoT devices remotely. In this section, we will explore how to integrate IoT technologies into your iOS applications.

Understanding IoT and Its Components

Before diving into the integration process, let's briefly understand the key components of IoT:

1. **IoT Devices:** These are physical objects equipped with sensors, actuators, and connectivity capabilities. Examples include smart thermostats, wearable fitness trackers, and connected light bulbs.
2. **IoT Platforms:** These platforms provide the infrastructure and tools to manage, analyze, and visualize data from IoT devices. Common IoT platforms include AWS IoT, Google Cloud IoT Core, and Azure IoT Hub.
3. **Connectivity Protocols:** IoT devices communicate with the cloud and each other using various connectivity protocols, such as Wi-Fi, Bluetooth, Zigbee, LoRa, and cellular networks.

Steps to Integrate IoT into Your iOS App

To integrate IoT functionality into your iOS app, follow these general steps:

1. Identify Your Use Case:

Start by defining the specific use case for IoT integration. Determine how IoT devices can enhance the user experience or provide valuable data.

2. Choose an IoT Platform:

Select an IoT platform that suits your project's requirements. Evaluate factors like scalability, data security, and compatibility with your IoT devices.

3. Develop a Backend Solution:

Create a backend system that can communicate with IoT devices. This system should handle data ingestion, storage, and device management.

4. Implement Device Authentication:

Ensure that your iOS app can securely authenticate and communicate with IoT devices. Implement authentication mechanisms like API keys or OAuth tokens.

5. Create the iOS App:

Develop the iOS app interface and user experience. Integrate IoT functionality into the app's interface, allowing users to control and monitor IoT devices.

6. Establish Data Communication:

Implement communication protocols between your iOS app and the IoT platform. Use APIs or SDKs provided by the IoT platform to send and receive data.

7. Real-Time Monitoring:

Provide real-time monitoring features within your app, allowing users to receive updates and notifications from their IoT devices.

8. User Authorization:

Implement user authorization and access control to ensure that users can only control their authorized IoT devices.

Sample Code Snippet

Here is a simplified code snippet demonstrating how to interact with an IoT device using HTTP requests in Swift:

```swift
import Foundation

let deviceId = "your_device_id"

let apiKey = "your_api_key"
```

```swift
let apiUrl = "https://api.iotplatform.com/device/\(deviceId)/control"

func controlIoTDevice() {

guard let url = URL(string: apiUrl) else {

print("Invalid URL")

return

}

var request = URLRequest(url: url)

request.httpMethod = "POST"

request.addValue("application/json", forHTTPHeaderField: "Content-Type")

request.addValue(apiKey, forHTTPHeaderField: "Authorization")

let command = ["command": "turn_on"]

guard let httpBody = try? JSONSerialization.data(withJSONObject: command) else {

print("Failed to create HTTP body")

return

}

request.httpBody = httpBody

let task = URLSession.shared.dataTask(with: request) { (data, response, error) in

if let error = error {
```

```swift
print("Error: \(error)")

} else if let data = data {

let responseString = String(data: data, encoding: .utf8)

print("Response: \(responseString ?? "")")

}

}

task.resume()

}
```

Use Cases for IoT Integration

Integrating IoT into your iOS app opens up various possibilities, including:

- **Smart Home Control:** Allow users to control smart lights, thermostats, and security cameras.

- **Health and Fitness Monitoring:** Integrate with wearable devices for tracking health and fitness data.

- **Industrial IoT:** Monitor and control machinery and sensors in industrial settings.

- **Environmental Monitoring:** Collect data from environmental sensors for research or local weather information.

- **Asset Tracking:** Track the location and status of assets using IoT-enabled devices.

By carefully planning and implementing IoT integration, you can create iOS apps that provide valuable IoT-related features, making them more appealing and functional to users.

Section 19.5: Future Trends in iOS Development

As the field of iOS development continues to evolve rapidly, it's essential to keep an eye on emerging trends and technologies that may shape the future of app development. Staying informed about these trends can help you make informed decisions and remain competitive in the ever-changing landscape of iOS development. In this section, we will explore some of the future trends that are expected to impact iOS development.

1. SwiftUI Maturation

SwiftUI, Apple's declarative UI framework, has been gaining traction since its introduction. As it matures, SwiftUI is expected to become the primary choice for building user interfaces in iOS apps. Developers can look forward to more robust features, better performance, and increased support from Apple.

2. Augmented Reality (AR)

ARKit, Apple's augmented reality framework, has opened up exciting possibilities for AR app development. AR is expected to continue growing, with applications in gaming, education, retail, and more. The integration of AR glasses or headsets may further expand the AR ecosystem.

3. Machine Learning and Core ML

Machine learning (ML) is becoming increasingly accessible to iOS developers. Core ML, Apple's machine learning framework, will likely see improvements and enhancements. Developers can leverage ML for tasks like image recognition, natural language processing, and predictive analytics.

4. Cross-Platform Development

Cross-platform frameworks like Flutter and React Native are gaining popularity, allowing developers to build apps for multiple platforms simultaneously. While native development remains important, cross-platform solutions will continue to evolve and offer more seamless experiences.

5. Swift Package Manager (SPM)

Swift Package Manager is becoming the go-to tool for managing dependencies in Swift projects. It simplifies the process of adding libraries and packages to your app. Expect further enhancements and widespread adoption.

6. Privacy and Security

With increasing concerns about data privacy, Apple will likely introduce more stringent privacy measures and requirements for app developers. Staying compliant with privacy regulations and safeguarding user data will be paramount.

7. IoT Integration

IoT integration in iOS apps will continue to grow, with more devices and industries adopting IoT technology. Apps that can seamlessly connect and control IoT devices will be in high demand.

8. 5G Technology

The rollout of 5G networks will significantly impact mobile app development. High-speed and low-latency connections will enable new types of applications, such as augmented reality streaming and real-time multiplayer gaming.

9. App Clips

App Clips provide lightweight, on-demand app experiences without the need for full app installations. They can be accessed via QR codes, NFC tags, or web links. Developers can explore opportunities to create convenient App Clips for their apps.

10. Accessibility and Inclusivity

As accessibility awareness grows, app developers will need to focus on creating inclusive experiences for all users. This includes designing apps for people with disabilities and ensuring compatibility with assistive technologies.

11. Swift Concurrency

Swift is expected to introduce new concurrency features that make it easier to write efficient and responsive code. This will simplify asynchronous programming and help apps take full advantage of multi-core processors.

12. Continuous Integration/Continuous Deployment (CI/CD)

Streamlining the development pipeline **with** CI/CD practices will become even more crucial. Automation **and** testing will help developers deliver high-quality apps faster **and with** fewer issues.

In conclusion, the future of iOS development holds exciting opportunities and challenges. By staying informed, adopting new technologies, and focusing on user-centric design, developers can thrive in this dynamic environment and create innovative and successful iOS apps. Keep exploring, learning, and adapting to the evolving landscape of iOS development to remain at the forefront of the industry.

Chapter 20: The Developer's Career

Section 20.1: Building a Portfolio

Building a strong portfolio is a crucial step in advancing your career as an iOS developer. Whether you're just starting or looking to take the next step in your professional journey, a well-crafted portfolio can make a significant difference. In this section, we will explore the importance of a developer's portfolio and provide guidance on how to create an impressive one.

Why Is a Portfolio Important?

Your portfolio serves as a visual representation of your skills, experience, and accomplishments. It's a showcase of the work you've done and the projects you've completed. Here's why having a portfolio is essential:

1. **Demonstrates Your Skills:** A portfolio allows you to demonstrate your technical skills, problem-solving abilities, and creativity to potential employers or clients.
2. **Builds Trust:** When applying for a job or freelance work, a portfolio can build trust with those considering your services. Seeing your past projects can reassure them of your capabilities.
3. **Highlights Your Achievements:** It provides a platform to highlight your achievements, such as apps you've developed, contributions to open-source projects, or any awards or recognitions you've received.

Differentiates

Section 20.2: Networking and Community Involvement

Networking and community involvement are essential aspects of advancing your career as an iOS developer. Building relationships, both online and offline, can lead to valuable opportunities, collaborations, and professional growth. In this section, we will explore the significance of networking and community engagement in your developer career.

Why Networking Matters

Networking is not just about collecting business cards or LinkedIn connections; it's about building meaningful relationships within the iOS development community. Here's why networking is crucial:

1. **Opportunity Discovery:** Networking exposes you to job opportunities, freelance gigs, and potential collaborations. Many opportunities are shared within professional networks before they are publicly advertised.
2. **Knowledge Sharing:** Interacting with peers allows you to exchange knowledge, learn from others, and stay updated on the latest trends and technologies in iOS development.
3. **Mentorship:** Networking can connect you with experienced professionals who can serve as mentors, offering guidance and insights to help you grow in your career.
4. **Support System:** Building a network provides you with a support system of like-minded individuals who understand the challenges and successes of the iOS development field.
5. **Visibility:** Active networking can increase your visibility in the industry. Sharing your knowledge and experiences through talks, blog posts, or open-source contributions can

make you a recognized figure.

How to Network Effectively

Effective networking involves more than just collecting contacts; it's about building and nurturing relationships. Here are some strategies to network effectively:

1. **Attend Events:** Participate in iOS-related events, such as conferences, meetups, and workshops. These events provide opportunities to meet industry professionals face-to-face.
2. **Online Communities:** Join online forums, discussion groups, and social media platforms where iOS developers gather. Contribute to discussions and share your expertise.
3. **Contribute to Open Source:** Collaborating on open-source projects not only demonstrates your skills but also connects you with other developers.
4. **Start a Blog or Podcast:** Share your insights and experiences by starting a blog, podcast, or YouTube channel. This can establish you as an authority in your niche.
5. **Speak at Conferences:** Consider presenting talks or workshops at conferences. Speaking engagements can help you gain recognition and credibility.
6. **Offer Help:** Be willing to assist others in the community. Answer questions, provide feedback, and mentor junior developers.
7. **Use LinkedIn Effectively:** Maintain an active and professional LinkedIn profile. Connect with industry professionals and engage with their content.
8. **Follow Up:** After meeting someone, follow up with a thank-you message or request for further discussion. Stay

in touch to maintain the relationship.

Joining Developer Communities

Being part of developer communities is an excellent way to network and stay connected. Here are a few iOS-related communities to consider:

1. **Apple Developer Forums:** Apple's official developer forums are a valuable resource for technical discussions and issue resolution.
2. **Stack Overflow:** Participate in iOS-related questions and answers on Stack Overflow. Providing helpful answers can boost your reputation.
3. **GitHub:** Contribute to open-source iOS projects on GitHub and collaborate with other developers.
4. **iOS Developer Slack Groups:** Many Slack communities are dedicated to iOS development. These provide a platform for real-time discussions.
5. **Twitter:** Follow iOS developers, bloggers, and influencers on Twitter. Engage in conversations using relevant hashtags.

Remember that networking is a long-term investment in your career. It may take time to see the full benefits, but the connections you build and the knowledge you gain will be invaluable throughout your journey as an iOS developer.

Section 20.3: Finding Job Opportunities

Finding job opportunities as an iOS developer can be an exciting and challenging endeavor. Whether you're looking for your first job in the field or aiming to advance your career, this section provides guidance on how to effectively search for job openings and secure your dream iOS development job.

Job Search Strategies

1. Online Job Portals: Use popular job portals such as LinkedIn, Indeed, Glassdoor, and Stack Overflow Jobs to search for iOS developer positions. These platforms allow you to filter job listings based on location, experience level, and other criteria.

2. Company Websites: Explore the career pages of companies you admire. Many organizations post job openings directly on their websites, which may not be available elsewhere.

3. Professional Networks: Leverage your professional network, including LinkedIn connections and contacts you've made through networking events or conferences. Informing your network about your job search can lead to referrals and recommendations.

4. Recruitment Agencies: Consider working with recruitment agencies that specialize in tech and IT placements. They often have access to exclusive job opportunities and can help match you with the right position.

5. GitHub and Open Source Contributions: If you have a strong GitHub profile with contributions to open-source projects, you may attract job offers from companies seeking developers with demonstrated skills.

6. Freelancing Platforms: Platforms like Upwork and Toptal offer freelance iOS development projects. Freelancing can be a way to build your portfolio and gain experience.

Crafting Your Application

1. Tailored Resumes: Customize your resume for each job application. Highlight relevant skills, experiences, and projects that align with the specific job description.

2. Cover Letters: Write compelling cover letters that explain why you are a good fit for the role. Address the company's needs and show your enthusiasm for the position.

3. Portfolio and GitHub: Include links to your portfolio website and GitHub profile on your resume. Showcase your projects, code samples, and contributions to demonstrate your abilities.

4. Online Presence: Ensure your LinkedIn profile is up to date and professional. Many employers review candidates' online profiles during the hiring process.

5. References: Prepare a list of professional references who can vouch for your skills and work ethic. Seek permission from these individuals beforehand.

Interview Preparation

1. Technical Skills: Brush up on your technical skills, including coding, problem-solving, and knowledge of iOS development frameworks and tools. Be prepared to demonstrate your abilities during technical interviews or coding tests.

2. Behavioral Questions: Practice answering common behavioral questions related to teamwork, conflict resolution, and communication. Use the STAR (Situation, Task, Action, Result) method to structure your responses.

3. Company Research: Research the companies you're interviewing with. Understand their products, culture, and mission. Tailor your responses to show how you align with their values and goals.

4. Questions for Interviewers: Prepare questions to ask the interviewers. This shows your interest in the role and the company. Ask about the team, project, and company's future plans.

5. Mock Interviews: Consider participating in mock interviews with a mentor or through online platforms. Practice will boost your confidence.

Job Offer Evaluation

1. Salary and Benefits: Evaluate the compensation package, including salary, bonuses, and benefits like health insurance, retirement plans, and stock options. Negotiate if necessary.

2. Company Culture: Assess the company's culture, work environment, and values. Ensure they align with your preferences and career goals.

3. Career Growth: Discuss opportunities for career advancement, skill development, and ongoing learning. A job should offer a path for growth.

4. Location and Commute: Consider the job location and

commute. Factor in the convenience and lifestyle implications.

5. Timeline: Review the expected start date and any probationary periods. Ensure they align with your availability.

Remember that the job search process can be competitive, and rejection is part of the journey. Stay persistent, keep improving your skills, and leverage your network to increase your chances of landing your ideal iOS development job.

Section 20.4: Freelancing and Entrepreneurship

In the world of iOS development, there's a significant opportunity for freelancers and entrepreneurs to thrive. Whether you want to work on projects independently or build your own app-based business, this section provides insights into freelancing and entrepreneurship in the iOS development domain.

Freelancing in iOS Development

1. Building Your Portfolio: Before diving into freelancing, build a strong portfolio of iOS projects. Having a collection of diverse and well-executed apps will help attract potential clients.

2. Selecting Niche Areas: Specialize in specific areas of iOS development, such as gaming, healthcare, or e-commerce. Clients often seek experts in particular niches.

3. Market Yourself: Create a professional website or online portfolio to showcase your skills and previous work. Use social media and online platforms like Upwork, Freelancer, or Toptal to market your services.

4. Pricing Strategies: Decide on your pricing structure. You can charge hourly rates or offer fixed-price contracts. Be transparent with clients about your rates and billing methods.

5. Contracts and Agreements: Always use contracts when working with clients. Clearly define project scope, timelines, payment terms, and deliverables to avoid misunderstandings.

6. Client Communication: Effective communication is crucial. Keep clients updated on project progress, address their concerns promptly, and set realistic expectations.

7. Time Management: Freelancers must manage their time effectively to balance multiple projects. Tools like project management software and time tracking apps can be helpful.

8. Feedback and Reviews: Encourage clients to provide feedback and reviews. Positive testimonials can boost your reputation and attract more clients.

Entrepreneurship in iOS Development

1. Idea Generation: Entrepreneurial iOS developers often start with a unique app idea. Research the market to identify needs and gaps that your app can address.

2. Business Plan: Create a detailed business plan that outlines your app's concept, target audience, monetization strategy, and marketing plan.

3. Development Team: Consider whether you'll develop the app solo or assemble a team. Collaborating with designers, marketers, and testers can enhance your app's quality.

4. Funding: Determine how you'll fund your startup. Options include personal savings, loans, angel investors, or crowdfunding platforms.

5. App Development: Follow best practices in iOS app development. Focus on user experience, performance, and security. Test thoroughly before launch.

6. App Monetization: Decide how you'll generate revenue, whether through ads, in-app purchases, subscriptions, or a one-time purchase. Your monetization model should align with your target audience.

7. Marketing and Promotion: Develop a marketing strategy to create awareness about your app. Utilize social media, app store optimization (ASO), and online advertising.

8. App Store Submission: Follow the guidelines of the App Store and Google Play Store for submission. Prepare promotional materials, screenshots, and app descriptions.

9. User Feedback: Gather user feedback and continuously improve your app based on user reviews and suggestions.

10. Scaling and Growth: As your app gains users, focus on scaling and expanding your business. Consider updates, new features, and potential partnerships.

Whether you choose freelancing or entrepreneurship, the iOS development field offers opportunities for those willing to invest in their skills and ideas. Both paths require dedication, creativity, and a commitment to delivering high-quality solutions to clients or users.

Section 20.5: Continuous Learning and Development

In the ever-evolving world of iOS development, the importance of continuous learning and professional development cannot be overstated. Staying up-to-date with the latest technologies, tools, and best practices is essential for a successful and fulfilling career in this field. This section explores the significance of continuous learning and provides guidance on how to keep your skills sharp and relevant.

The Rapid Evolution of iOS Development

iOS development is characterized by its rapid evolution. Apple regularly releases new versions of iOS, Xcode, and Swift, each bringing a host of features, improvements, and changes. To keep up with these updates and take full advantage of the platform, developers must invest in continuous learning.

Ways to Continuously Improve Your iOS Development Skills

1. Online Courses and Tutorials: Numerous online platforms offer iOS development courses and tutorials. Websites like Udemy, Coursera, edX, and Pluralsight provide access to a wide range of courses, from beginner to advanced levels.

2. Official Documentation: Apple's official documentation is a valuable resource. It provides in-depth information about iOS SDKs, frameworks, and best practices. Regularly refer to it to deepen your understanding.

3. Books and eBooks: Invest in iOS development books authored by experts. Books provide comprehensive insights into various aspects of iOS development and often include practical examples.

4. iOS Development Blogs: Follow blogs and websites dedicated to iOS development. These platforms frequently share tutorials, tips, and news related to the iOS ecosystem.

5. Conferences and Meetups: Attend iOS development conferences and local meetups. These events offer opportunities to learn from industry leaders, network with peers, and gain exposure to emerging trends.

6. Open Source Contributions: Contribute to open source iOS projects. This not only allows you to give back to the community but also provides hands-on experience with real-world codebases.

7. Online Communities: Join iOS development communities on platforms like GitHub, Stack Overflow, and Reddit. Engage in discussions, seek help when needed, and share your knowledge with others.

8. Side Projects: Work on personal side projects to apply and reinforce your skills. Building your own apps or libraries can be an excellent way to learn and experiment.

9. Mentorship: Consider finding a mentor or becoming a mentor to someone else. Mentorship can provide guidance, accountability, and valuable insights.

10. Certifications: Pursue iOS development certifications if relevant to your career goals. These certifications can validate your expertise and make you more competitive in the job market.

Embracing Change and Adaptation

In the dynamic field of iOS development, adaptability is a key asset. Embrace change as an opportunity to learn and grow. Be open to exploring new technologies, design patterns, and development methodologies. As you gain experience, you'll develop a deeper understanding of the iOS ecosystem, enabling you to adapt to changes with greater ease.

Conclusion

Continuous learning is not just a professional responsibility; it's a means to thrive and excel in the iOS development industry. By staying curious, investing in your education, and actively participating in the iOS community, you can ensure that your skills remain relevant and that you continue to deliver innovative and high-quality solutions to users worldwide. Remember that learning is a lifelong journey, and the more you invest in it, the more you'll reap the rewards in your iOS development career.